Practical Studies in Systematic Design

Practical Studies
in Systematic Design

Vladimir Hubka
Institut für Konstruktion und Bauweise, Eidenössische Technische Hochschule, Zurich, Switzerland

M Myrup Andreasen
Instituttet for Konstruktiensteknik, Danmarks Tekniske Højskole, Lyngby, Denmark

W Ernst Eder
Department of Mechanical Engineering, Royal Military College of Canada, Kingston, Ontario, Canada

Advisory Editor
Peter Hills
Head of Design Group, The Royal Military College of Science, Shrivenham, Wiltshire, England

Butterworths
London Boston Sydney Wellington Durban Toronto

First published 1988

© **Butterworth & Co. (Publishers) Ltd, 1988**

British Library Cataloguing-in-Publication Data

Hubka, Vladimir
  Practical studies in systematic design.
  1. Engineering. Design
  I. Title II. Andreasen, M. Myrup
  (Mogens Myrup)
  620′.00425

  ISBN 0-408-01420-2

Library of Congress Cataloguing-in-Publication Data

Hubka, Vladimir
  Practical studies in systematic design/Vladimir
Hubka, M. Myrup Andreasen, W. Ernst Eder.
    p. cm.
  Bibliography: p.
  Includes index.
  ISBN 0-408-01420-2:
  1. Engineering design. I. Andreasen,
M.M. (Mogens Myrup), 1939– II. Eder, W.E.
(Wolfgang Ernst) III. Title.
TA174.H83 1988
620′.00425—dc19   88-10594

Typeset at the Alden Press Oxford London and
Northampton
Printed and bound in Great Britain by Anchor Brendon
Ltd., Tiptree, Essex

Preface

Despite the abundance of literature on systematic design and design methods, there is a distinct lack of suitable case studies and examples that adequately demonstrate the design process. To be of value to the student and the engineering designer, such case studies should follow the process of designing a device, step by step, from the initial recognition of a need to a manufacturable product.

No current book contains examples that demonstrate all stages of the process of systematically designing a technical system and also illustrate the effects of applying known methods and procedures. One reason for this is the difficulty of finding problems that can be easily understood by a wide range of readers but at the same time clarify the design process for the expert in a convincing way in spite of the simplifications necessary. One must be wary about criticisms that arise from such attempts to simplify and explain the procedures, and it is readily accepted that many of the decisions reached within the design examples included in this book may not meet with unanimous agreement because of the simplifications used.

However, studies and design examples are invaluable to students and engineers, despite these possible shortcomings. Aims for such examples are:

● to aid the understanding and application of a systematic approach during engineering design work, both for the practising designer and for the student
● to provide a basis for discussion of design methodology for engineering experts and scholars
● to serve as a source of stimulus and as a teaching aid for teachers of engineering design.

Each engineering design problem must pass through various stages from the recognition of a need, and considerations of how the design objectives could be achieved, to laying out the mechanisms and devices in drawings that are progressively closer to the future product, and then progressing to full manufacturing information. A systematic design procedure should encompass all stages of all possible design problems. It should allow the designer sufficient freedom to use and enhance experience and creativity, and should permit the use of judgement by omitting stages in the process that are considered unnecessary for the particular problem in hand.

Many engineers prefer to read drawings and diagrams rather than pure text. The design studies presented in this book make extensive use of such graphical representations, and thus provide a readily understandable set of examples of methodical design.

The aims stated above, coupled with a desire for clarity, resulted in the selection of the examples included in this volume. These are all simple technical systems with easily understood purposes and modes of action. The emphasis in these design studies is placed on the phases leading to the dimensional layout, and particularly on establishing the technical process (TP) and the concepts of a proposed technical system (TS).

This work was undertaken within the Workshop Design-Konstruktion (WDK) organization, and follows the WDK system. Consequently the examples in this collection fit firmly into the framework of the General Procedural Model of Engineering Design, as presented in *Principles of Engineering Design* by V. Hubka (translated and edited by W.E. Eder), published by Butterworths in 1982, and referred to in the text as *Principles* [1]. Nevertheless, the authors have tried to clarify the steps of the design process within the examples so that this book can be used as a text in its own right, or to complement other books on engineering design.

Thanks are due to Peter Hills, The Royal Military College of Science, Shrivenham, in his capacity as Advisory Editor, for his many stimulating comments on the manuscript.

V. Hubka
M. Myrup Andreasen
W. Ernst Eder

Contents

Note   Costs and prices as estimated at the time when
the case studies were first written are stated in various
currencies. The exchange rates were approximately:
£100 = DKr 1300 = SwFr 300 = Can$190 =
US$155

Key to graphic symbols

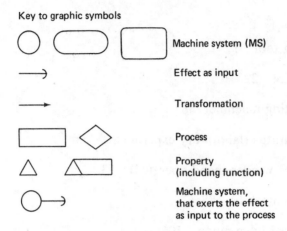

Machine system (MS)

Effect as input

Transformation

Process

Property
(including function)

Machine system,
that exerts the effect
as input to the process

Introduction

The design case studies in this volume show examples of the activities of engineering designers, using systematic methods. They have been edited as far as possible into a uniform format to emphasize the consistent nature of design, to provide a good overview, and to enhance understanding. This introduction contains a number of hints to help the reader in working through the case studies.

Theory and background

The design studies presented here are in the form described in *Principles* [1], based on the WDK methods and the general *Theory of Technical Systems* [2]. If this book is used with other texts on engineering design, some adjustment will be needed to accommodate the different approaches and terminology.

Design methodology aims to give the designer a model, procedure or strategy for design work and to increase the probability of achieving a successful solution. A model design process should be as comprehensive and general as possible, to accommodate many different problems. These may range over designing a completely new device, creating a competitive product, redesigning an existing product, and even making minor changes. The designer must have the freedom within the general methodology to choose appropriate tactics, to use any available method or aid, to omit any step in the procedure, and to return to a previous step to review, augment or revise. The general aim should be to complete each step before starting the next. However, some overlapping (in time) of the steps and stages in the iterative process of designing is usual, and frequently unavoidable as additional information relating to earlier steps is generated in subsequent work.

One aim of these case studies is to demonstrate that a systematic procedure need not reduce creativity, but can enhance it by providing a framework and orientation for original thought. Each step in the design process consists of a series of identifiable stages. Good preparation for objective and goal-oriented creative work needs a thorough, systematic investigation of the problem and its implications. Creativity must be supplemented by thorough verification. Systematic design procedures must be flexible enough not to impede any individual's approach to design.

The General Procedural Model of the Design Process shown in Figure 0-1 [1] forms the basis for setting up a procedural plan (the systematic design approach to a particular problem, given the likely complexity of the technical system and the difficulty of the design task), and deriving from it a mode of working suited to the preferences and capabilities of the designer. The stepwise progression of this model was derived by Hubka in *Theory of Design Processes* [3], and the individual steps receive their justification in *Theory of Technical Systems* [2].

During the design process, the state of a technical system depends on a sequence of transformations and is described by a number of design characteristics. The transformations involve the processing of information as the design moves from the abstract to the concrete. The design characteristics are represented by written, mathematical or graphical descriptions in various design documents. These can take on a variety of forms [4, 5], depending on the immediate purpose and content of the information.

Systematic progress in design is based on generating and varying design characteristics, which are treated as classifying and ordering relationships. The context in which the states of a technical system, the established design characteristics and the design documents co-exist is illustrated in Figure 0-2.

The designer usually aims to formulate the conditions which should lead to an optimal solution, a best compromise all things considered. Many optima are relatively insensitive to changes in design variables, and there may exist a number of local optima. In the early stages of the design process a choice of an optimal solution can be difficult and is not obvious. There is no single right answer, and differences of opinion on choices may be expected and will change as the designer becomes more familiar with the problem.

A systematic design methodology should encourage the designer to keep good records, and to make each step and thought retrievable as representations on paper or other suitable media, not subject to the vagaries of human memory. In this way earlier thoughts and decisions can be reviewed, steps can be retracted and modified as new information becomes available, and the project and its design process can be more easily managed by the designer and project management.

Every decision has some effect on the following phases of the project, and, in general, the earlier the decision the more pronounced the effect on

Figure 0-1

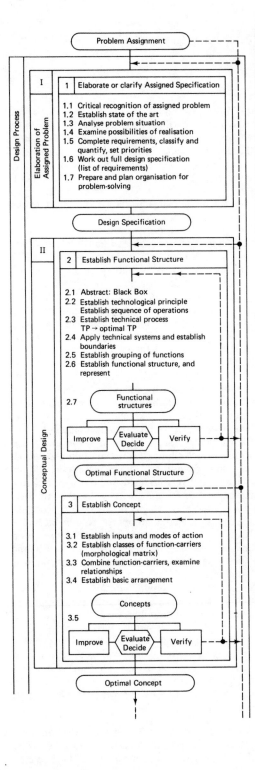

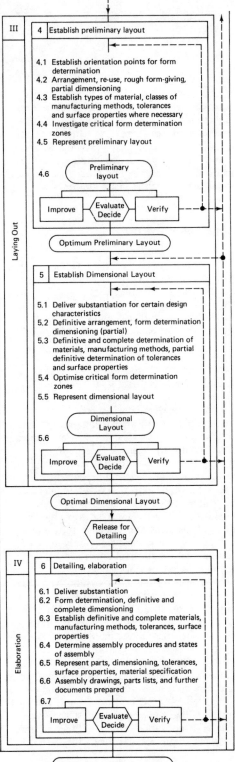

Figure 0-2

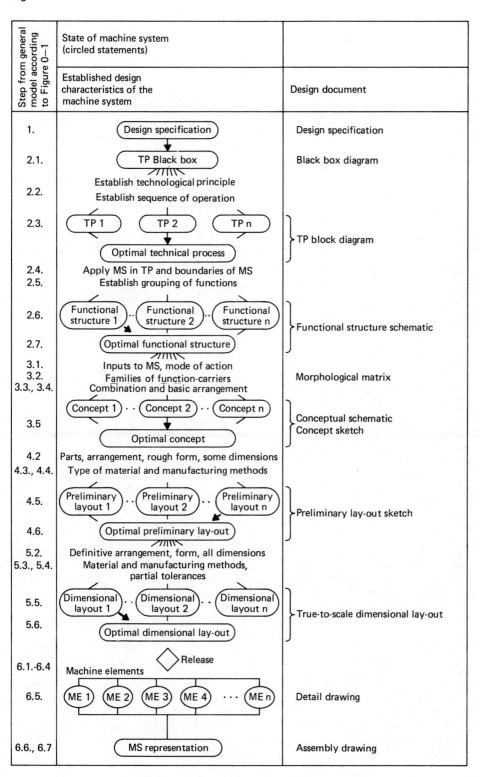

Step from general model according to Figure 0—1	State of machine system (circled statements)	
	Established design characteristics of the machine system	Design document
1.	Design specification	Design specification
2.1.	TP Black box	Black box diagram
2.2.	Establish technological principle / Establish sequence of operation	
2.3.	TP 1 TP 2 TP n / Optimal technical process	TP block diagram
2.4. / 2.5.	Apply MS in TP and boundaries of MS / Establish grouping of functions	
2.6.	Functional structure 1 .. Functional structure 2 .. Functional structure n	Functional structure schematic
2.7.	Optimal functional structure	
3.1. / 3.2. / 3.3., 3.4.	Inputs to MS, mode of action / Families of function-carriers / Combination and basic arrangement	Morphological matrix
3.5	Concept 1 ·· Concept 2 ·· Concept n / Optimal concept	Conceptual schematic / Concept sketch
4.2 / 4.3., 4.4.	Parts, arrangement, rough form, some dimensions / Type of material and manufacturing methods	
4.5.	Preliminary layout 1 .. Preliminary layout 2 .. Preliminary layout n	Preliminary lay-out sketch
4.6.	Optimal preliminary lay-out	
5.2. / 5.3., 5.4.	Definitive arrangement, form, all dimensions / Material and manufacturing methods, partial tolerances	
5.5.	Dimensional layout 1 .. Dimensional layout 2 .. Dimensional layout n	True-to-scale dimensional lay-out
5.6.	Optimal dimensional lay-out	
6.1.-6.4	Release / Machine elements	
6.5.	ME 1 ME 2 ME 3 ME 4 ··· ME n	Detail drawing
6.6., 6.7.	MS representation	Assembly drawing

performance. It is often observed that there is a tendency for the effects of decisions to be amplified rather than attenuated with the passing of time. [6]

Good record-keeping aids communication, both inside and outside the design team [7].

Form of the design studies and type of representation

The procedure used for each individual design study is shown in a diagram similar to Figure 0-2 placed at the start of each case. The figure gives an overview of the scope and steps of that particular case study. The numbers attached to each of the design documents (the figures in the case study) are entered into this scheme opposite the relevant step.

The general procedure follows the set of steps from *Principles* [1], and uses the headings as shown in Figure 0-1. Each step involves the authors' answers to one or more of the following:

● Aim of the particular step or sequence of steps
● Starting documents (usually the documents from the immediately preceding step, but considering all work leading up the current step)
● Method (tactics, sequence of actions and thoughts by the designer to fulfil the aims of a step)
● Assumptions and simplifications
● Aids to creative work
● Decisions, and reasons for choices
● Results of the designer's (or design team's) work, and comments with respect to effectiveness, deviations from the model, etc.

These examples provide an insight into a general strategy, a General Procedural Model of Engineering Design. Awareness of such a general strategy, and of the methods actually used by the designer, is more important than slavishly following a set of rules. The general procedure should allow the design engineer to control, guide, regulate, check and alter the flow of work towards a solution.

Design is a human activity and depends on creativity, knowledge and experience, among other factors. The designer must try to assess the likely benefits of all design strategies and tactics, in order to explain what they contain and why they are likely to work. The cases in this volume illustrate these and associated activities.

Each of the case studies shows that the designer (or design team) has performed a large amount of work, including trials, false starts, re-thinking, attaining new insights, revisions, re-drawing, etc. These cases indicate the scope of this work by showing some of the intermediate stages, presenting the outcome at the end of each step, and discussing some of the points involved in a systematic approach to the design of a technical system.

Terminology, symbols

In order to understand the explanations in this book, it is necessary to understand the theory as presented in *Principles* [1]. Brief summaries may be found in references 8 and 9, which also include some background from reference 2. Terminology in the examples is as consistent as possible, and the words are used in the senses defined in the Glossary of *Principles* [1], and in reference 10. Each word has a definite and consistent meaning that usually does not embrace the full range and possible ambiguity of meanings attached to it in common usage. Some of the terminology may appear laboured, but the aim is to keep different usages apart, so that overall clarity can be achieved. Examples of such usage are:

Design The activity of designing (but not the end-result).

Socio-technical system A composite of physical and social elements and their interactions, consisting of technical processes plus technical systems plus human beings plus the environment.

Technical system A composite of physical elements and their interactions, which receives inputs, and delivers effects to guide and drive a technical process.

Function The duty of a technical system to deliver specified effects at its output.

Mode of action The internal way in which a technical system performs its tasks to accept commands and inputs, and exerts effects on a technical process.

Action location The place at which a technical system receives its inputs (a receptor), or delivers its effects (an effector).

Design characteristic Those sizes, forms, action principles, functions, performance values, arrangements, etc. that influence the constructional solution, and are established, selected and decided by the designer to characterize the technical system that is intended to help in solving the problem.

Process That which transforms an operand from one state to another (preferably more desirable) state.

Operand The material, energy and/or information that is being transformed in the technical process, throughput of a system.

Operation A part of a transformation process that is not usefully sub-divided.

Operator Any thing (usually a technical system) or person that delivers effects to guide and drive a technical process.

Technology The interaction of a technical system with a technical process (analogous to the interaction of a tool and a workpiece), or how the effects (output) of a technical system or human being act to guide and drive a technical process or an operation within it.

Figure 0-3   Summary of steps and illustrations in cases

E   explanation of general procedure or theory
S   progress of step used in case study
C   comment on progress of case study
R   review of step at later stage
D   step used for details of a sub-system
F   figures referred to in progress of step
T   tables referred to in progress of step
| combined discussion of steps or explanations (see next symbol in column)

Steps from General Model according to Figure 0.1	Step	Case 1	Case 2	Case 3	Case 4	Case 5	Case 6	Case 7	Case 8
1 Aim: elaborate or clarify the assigned specification	1.1	E |C F	F	S	S F	| F	S	|	F
	1.2	E |	F	S	S	|	S	|	|
	1.3	E S		S	E S	|	S	S F	|
	1.4	E S	E C	S	E S TF	S	S	S F	|
	1.5	E |C	|	|	|	|	S	S F	|
	1.6	E S F	E S F	S F	S R TF	S F	S F	S F	S F
	1.7	E S F	E S F	S F	S	S	S		S
2 Aim: establish the functional structures	2.1	E S F	E S F	S | F	S F	S F	S F		|
	2.2	E S F	S F	S R| F	E S F	S F	S F		|
	2.3	E S F	E S F	E S R| F	S F	S F	S R F		|
	2.4	E S F	S F	| | F	S	S	|		|
	2.5	E C	C	S |	S F	S	|		C
	2.6	E S F	E S F	S | F	E S F	S F	S F		E S F
	2.7	E |C		S D	S			S R	
3 Aim: establish the concepts	3.1	E |	C	|	S	S			S
	3.2	E S F	S F	|	S F	S F		S F	E S F
	3.3	E |	S	|	E S F	S F	S R F	S |	S F
	3.4	E S F	S F	| F	S F	S F	E S R F	S R F	E S F
	3.5	E S F	S F	E C D F	E	S F	S R F	S F	S F
4 Aim: establish the preliminary layouts	4.1	E S F	S	D	S F		S F	|	C
	4.2	E C	|	D F			S F	S	
	4.3	E C	C	D			|	|	
	4.4	E S	C	D			S F	S	
	4.5	E S F	S F	D F		S F	S F	|	
	4.6	E S	C			S F	S F	|	
5 Aim: establish the dimensional layouts	5.1	E C	|			S		|	S
	5.2	E	|			|		|	|
	5.3	E	|			|		|	|
	5.4	E S	|			|		|	S
	5.5	E S F	S F			S F		S F	S F
	5.6	E S F	S F						E S F
6 Aim: detailing, elaboration	6.1	|						S F	
	6.2	|							
	6.3	|							
	6.4	|							
	6.5	|							
	6.6	|							
	6.7	E C		F					

Method A general approach and advice to a designer (a controlled interaction between the human and a problem).

Procedure Specific rules and sequences of mental and physical human operations.

Technique The way of performing the mental or physical operations.

Optimum (a noun, and **optimal**, its adjective) A best compromise (which is not necessarily unique, since there may be a variety of opinions about how to make the compromise and about what should be considered important) to fufil a number of stated criteria under given constraints, under present conditions of knowledge, etc. Most optima are surrounded by an area of uncertainty in which deviations from the 'exact' value have a negligible effect on the outcome.

Concept A mental model (existing as a sketch) of a technical system; it includes the arrangements of major groupings of parts in outline form.

Represent Show, display, depict an existing or proposed technical system, its process, functions, organs, concepts, arrangements, constructional elements, etc. The process of establishing a model of the system in any appropriate medium such as cardboard or wood, pencil on paper, in computer memory, or by other means.

The diagrams and explanations make consistent use of symbols (both written and graphical) which are defined in the frontispiece figure.

Study procedure

This book contains eight cases studies in engineering design, each of which has particular features that are described in more detail at the start of each case. The following approach is suggested when reading this work:

- Read Case 1 to see a full application of the systematic procedure; study the explanations of the aims and methods used in each step.
- Read any or all cases: the sections preceding each case explain the significance of the text and the graphical illustrations.
- Study the basic procedure (see Figure 0-1), and make a parallel study of the same steps as actually executed by designers in the case studies.
- Study Case 3 as an in-depth discourse on the problem area of technical processes.
- Study Case 4, which illustrates the roles of data acquisition, approximate worst case calculations, and treatment of error quantities.

- Study the differences in the designers' approaches in these studies, depending on the nature of the problem, the amount and nature of the available information, and the capabilities, preferences, experiences and working methods of the individual design engineers. This includes deviations from the model (Case 3 onwards), and application of different design methods (*Principles*, Table 3, and reference 11), as decided by different designers.

Figure 0-3 shows which steps from the procedural model are explicitly used in each of the cases. In many instances where two or more headings from the Procedural Model appear in an uninterrupted block, some of the preceding steps may also influence the current work.

We wish you success, and welcome your comments and suggestions. We should like to hear of your experiences with systematic design.

References

1. HUBKA, V. *Principles of Engineering Design*, London, Butterworths (1982); reprinted Zürich, Heurista (1988)
2. HUBKA, V. *Theorie Technischer Systeme* (2nd edn), Berlin, Springer-Verlag (1983). English edition: HUBKA, V. and EDER, W.E. *Theory of Technical Systems*, New York, Springer-Verlag (1988)
3. HUBKA, V. *Theorie der Konstruktionsprozesse*, Berlin, Springer-Verlag (1975)
4. TJALVE, E., ANDREASEN, M.M. and SCHMIDT, F.F. *Engineering Graphic Modelling*, London, Butterworths (1979)
5. ANDREASEN, M.M. Darstellungsmöglichkeiten beim Konstruieren, *Schweizer Maschinenmarkt*, **78**, No. 4 & 6 (1978)
6. DARNELL, H. and DALE, M.W. Total Project Management – an integrated approach to the management of capital investment projects, *Proc. I. Mech. E.* **196**, No. 36, 337–346 (1982)
7. TURNER, B.T. Project engineering and the need for good communication, *CME*, **30**, No. 6, 36–38 (1983)
8. EDER, W.E. Structures as models in the design and development of a system, in IFIP W.G. 5.2 Tokyo 1985, *Design Theory for CAD*, H. Yoshikawa and E.A. Warman (eds), Amsterdam, Elsevier/North-Holland (1987), pp. 33–49
9. EDER, W.E. and HUBKA, V. Methodical design in engineering – basis and applicability, in *Cybernetics and Systems*, R. Trappl (ed.), Dordrecht, Reidel (1986), pp. 181–188
10. HUBKA, V. (ed.) *Fachbegriffe der wissenschaftlichen Konstruktionslehre in 6 Sprachen*, Zürich, Heurista (1981)
11. JONES, J.C. *Design methods – seeds of human futures* (2nd edn), New York, Wiley-Interscience (1980)

Case 1 Rivet setting tool

This case study shows the application of the systematic design method to a simple technical system, a hand-operated machine tool. The steps in the design process are shown in Figures 0-1 and 0-2. In this case study each step is first explained in principle, by means of the comments set in square brackets []. Immediately following these comments the design work, particularly the work of generating concepts for the rivet setting tool, is presented. .

Figure 1-1 surveys the procedure and refers to the design documents generated up to the dimensional layout (compare Figure 0-2). The designer has not departed significantly from the procedural model, but has omitted or combined some steps.

Introduction

A large car repair workshop needs a simple rivet setting tool. Need for five such tools is anticipated (with the possibility of sales to other users at a later date). This problem is assigned by the workshop management to a designer in a design consulting agency, who is required to produce a layout. The tool will be manufactured in the well equipped workshop facilities of the repair workshop, where there is a good range of machine tools. A reasonable level of finance is available.

The rivet setting tool is to be used for riveting linings to conventional (internal expanding drum) brake shoes. Details, dimensions and other data as supplied by the repair workshop are shown in Figure 1-2.

Problem assignment

[This **event** is the start of the design sequence. A sponsor (in this case the repair workshop) has **assigned** the problem to a designer.]

1. Aim: elaborate or clarify the assigned specification

[The aim of this sequence of **steps** is to generate a full design specification, namely:

(1) to expand the sponsor's statement of the problem in order to interpret what is wanted, and
(2) to add any information about possible constraints on the designer's work.

The result may be two different documents:

(a) a 'design specification' as part of a contract between sponsor and designer (in many cases this will take a standard form, even a legal document), and
(b) a 'list of requirements' for the designer's own reference which should be drawn up in an easily reviewed format.

Frequently the design engineer will propose answers to the problem immediately. A final formulation will usually not be reached until the ideas and work have been reviewed and revised a number of times. An overlap of steps is common, but should be avoided where possible. In the review process, the work done generally improves the designer's understanding of the problem.]

1.1 Critically recognize the assigned problem

[The aims are to study the assigned problem, to observe where and how the device is likely to be used, to discover any **implied facts** (possibly false ones) and **information** from other sources relevant to the problem or its solution, and to establish **value criteria** for deciding whether a proposal is likely to be adequate and for selecting between alternatives.]

In this case, the designer decides to combine this step with the next two.

1.2 Establish the state of the art

[The designer is encouraged to search in the literature (books, periodicals, trade information, etc.) to find out what similar problems have been solved, how, and at what costs.

This investigation will provide the designer with a background to the problem, but must not be permitted to inhibit the creative search for new solutions. For this reason it may be preferable to defer this step until steps 1.3 and 1.4 have been attempted.]

1.3 Analyse the problem situation

[The aim is to review the information gathered up to this point, and to add any new considerations that may have emerged.]

The designer is now familiar with the problem and has discussed it with the management of the repair workshop. Some catalogues listing similar tools have been obtained, from which the design engineer

Figure 1-1

Steps from General Model according to Figure 0.1	Step	Progress of case	Design documents
1 Aim: elaborate or clarify the assigned specification	1.1 1.2 1.3 1.4 1.5 1.6 1.7	Problem Assignment 1-2 1-3 1-4	Design Specification Timetable
2 Aim: establish the functional structures	2.1 2.2 2.3 2.4 2.5 2.6 2.7	1-5 1-6 1-7 1-8 1-9A 1-9B 1-9 1-9C	Black Box Diagram Technological Principle Technical Process Duties of Operator Functional Structures
3 Aim: establish the concepts	3.1 3.2 3.3 3.4 3.5	1-10 1-11 1-12 1-13 1-14 1-15 1-16 1-17 1-18 1-19, 1-20	Morphological Matrix } Concepts Evaluation Chart Relative Strength Diagr.
4 Aim: establish the preliminary layouts	4.1 4.2 4.3 4.4 4.5 4.6	1-21 1-14 1-15 1-18 1-23 1-22 1-24	Optimum Concept Preliminary Layouts
5 Aim: establish the dimensional layouts	5.1 5.2 5.3 5.4 5.5 5.6	1-25 1-26 1-27	Dimensional Layouts Evaluation Chart
6 Aim: detailing, elaboration	6.1 6.2 6.3 6.4 6.5 6.6 6.7	1-26	Optimum Layout

1-2 Problem Assignment

Design of a tool for riveting
brake linings onto brake
shoes for internal drum brakes

Internal Drum Brake:

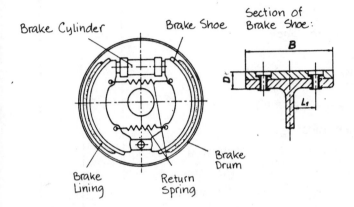

Brake Cylinder   Brake Shoe   Section of Brake Shoe:

Brake Lining   Return Spring   Brake Drum

Data:
- Brake drum - inside dia.:
   250 - 400 mm
- Rivet to DIN standard 7338
   shank dia.: 3-5 mm
   material: Cu
- max. shoe width: $100\,mm = B_{max}$
- max. total thickness of parts:
   $15\,mm = D_{max}$
- min. distance rivet ℄ from rib:
   $10\,mm = L_{1\,min}$
- Riveting stroke: ~ 3mm
- Riveting force: ~ 500 N
- manufacturing cost:
   less than SwFr 500·00

discovers that riveting tools for manual and mechanized operation are available from proprietary sources.

Visits to two other repair workshops give the designer a grasp of the technology of riveting brake linings. This experience and the information from the catalogues help the designer to understand the **state of the art** in this area.

1.4 Examine the possibilities of realization

[In this step, the designer aims to judge whether a solution is theoretically possible, whether a device can be designed and manufactured (**realized**) within the given constraints, and whether it can be economically justified. This assessment is necessarily approximate. Further work will be saved if it can be shown at this stage that such a device or solution is **not feasible**.]

Because this problem is fairly simple, the designer can be reasonably certain that a technical solution can be realized. Among the several solution proposals that can be generated there is likely to be at least one which can be made within the stated financial constraints.

1.5 Complete the requirements, classify and quantify, set priorities

[Any other factors that may affect a solution with respect to its evaluation, manufacture, etc. must now be considered. The collected statements can then be ordered into groups by reference to *Principles* (Figure 5), any numerical data clearly stated including their

range and accuracy, and decisions made about the priorities attached to each requirement.]

For this first case study, this step is combined with the following one.

1.6 Work out the full design specification (list of requirements)

[The aim here is to produce a complete, quantified list of requirements (design specification) with priorities, in written and diagrammatic form, to describe the problem, and to state clearly what a proposed solution should be able to *do*, and within what limits of performance it should operate. Statements of what a solution should *be* (in terms of hardware) are best avoided at this stage.

The designer can use the 'method of questioning', based on lists of classes of properties (*Principles*, Figure 5) and suitable questionnaires (*Principles*, p. 79).]

The starting documentation for this step includes the specification as given by the repair workshop to the designer, and the information collected and generated in the steps leading up to this point.

The result of the designer's work up to this point is shown as the design specification in Figure 1-3. This list is divided into a number of suitable categories to help the designer's further work. For the purposes of a contract with a customer the specification may need to be formalized in a different manner.

A noteworthy feature of the specification is the attempt to recognize all elements of the technical

1-3

Design Specification	PROJECT:	Fixed Req.	Desire
WDK Sheet 1/2	Rivet Setting Tool		

1. Function

Riveting of Brake Lining to Shoe   ×

2. Conditions of Techn. Process (TP)

2.1 Brake Shoe (Operand of the TP)   ×

a) Form and Dimensions:

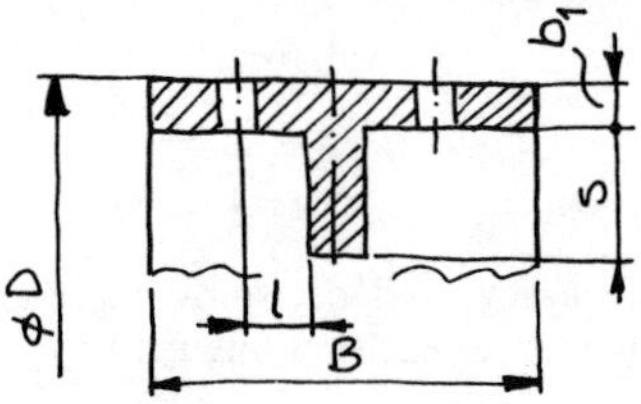

ϕD 250 – 400 mm
B   80 – 100 mm
b_1 6 – 8 mm
l_{min} 10 mm
β_{max} 150°
s_{max} 50 mm

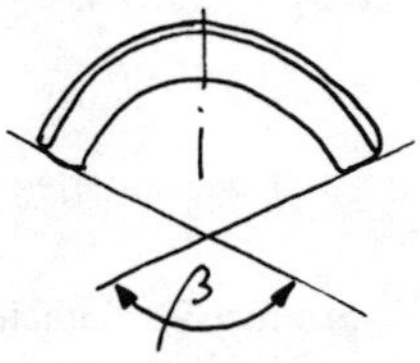

b) Material : Al-alloy
c) Mass: 2 kg max
d) State: cleaned, holes drilled
e) No. of Rivets : 10 – 16

2.2 Brake Lining (Operand of the TP)   ×

a) Form and Dimensions:

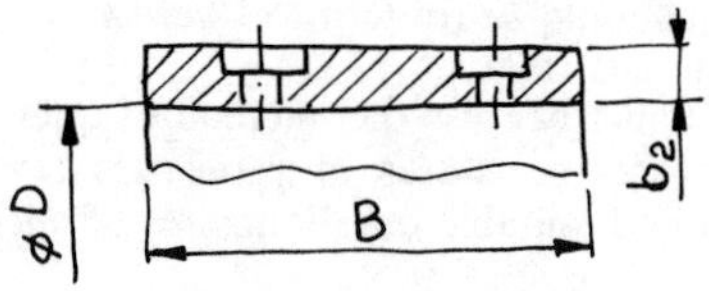

ϕD 250 – 400 mm
B   80 – 100 mm
b_2 6 – 8 mm

b) Material: Special Friction Lining
c) Mass: 200 g max
d) State: form pressed, holes drilled

2.3 Rivet   ×

a) Form and Dimension to DIN 7338
b) Mass: not relevant
c) State: annealed

1-3 Continued :

Design Specification		PROJECT: Rivet Setting Tool	Fixed Req.	Desire
WDK	Sheet 2/2			
		2.4 Riveting Procedure (TP)		
		a) Riveting Force ~ 500 N (experiment)	×	
		b) — Stroke (good closure) 4 mm	×	
		c) Capability ~ 70 Rivets/day	×	
		d) One-man Operation (car mechanic)	×	
		2.5 Environment (close)		
		a) Worktop, Material : wood		
		3. Operational Properties		
		3.1 Service Life 5 years	×	
		3.2 Good Transportability		×
		3.3 Reliable		×
		3.4 Maintenance Free		×
		4. Ergonomic Properties		
		4.1 Hand: force: 200 N or Foot: 400 N	×	
		4.2 Working Height · see Ergonomic Tables	×	
		4.3 Safety against accidents	×	
		5. Appearance No special requirements		
		6. Distribution, Storage		
		Good Storage friendliness (Volume)		×
		7. Delivery, Planning		
		Delivery deadline 3 months (4 max)	×	
		No. off ?	×	
		8. Manufacturing		
		Manufacturable in workshops of .... Co. Ltd	×	
		9. Costs		
		Manufacturing costs Sw Fr 400 max	×	

1-4 Timetable for problem

Activity :	Hours:	Gantt Chart :
1. Clarify and Establish Problem Statement, work out full Design Specification, Discussion with Contract Partner	ШШ	
2. Establishing Functional Structure	ШШ	
3. Establishing Concepts	ШШШ	
4. Preliminary Layouts, Discussion with Contract Partner, Dimensional Layout, Presentation	ШШ|	
Total	ШШ	

system, even if during subsequent design work some of the data may turn out to be redundant. This systematic description serves as an aid to a later, more complete analysis.

1.7   Prepare and plan for problem-solving

[The main goal of this step is to plan the problem-solving and its organization in an attempt to predict how the project is to be managed. From the designer's point of view, the requirement is to adjust the sequence of design steps into a plan suited to the particular problem, then to consider the timetable and deadlines, and to plan the facilities needed to ensure progress.]

Because the technical system to be designed is simple, the complete process (as shown in Figure 0-1) is not necessary, but has been retained in this description to clarify the individual steps. The emphasis in this design task is on establishing the mode of action for the technical system that is proposed as the solution to the processing problem.

A timetable is set up by the designer, and is shown in Figure 1-4. A special, more detailed procedural plan is not considered necessary.

Design specification

[The second event in the design sequence is submission of the completed design specification to the sponsor, and obtaining approval if necessary.]

2   Aim: establish the functional structures

[The aim of this sequence of steps is to recognize the effects needed from a *technical system* (TS), so that it can guide and drive the *technical processes* (TP) required by the specification. These effects can only be produced if the system performs certain functions, and if these functions are structured in an appropriate way. The designer should ideally generate some alternative process descriptions, functions etc., and in a separate procedure should evaluate and decide between them.]

2.1   Abstract: produce the black box representations

[By careful study of all the requirements the aim is to recognize and formulate clearly in abstract terms the transformations that are necessary to ensure that the operands achieve the desired final state, i.e. to abstract from the given information, avoiding references to existing hardware or software, if possible. These transformations contain information about the technical process, and some of the information about the functions of the technical system (TS) to be designed.]

A 'black box' diagram of riveting, as a conventional representation of the process to be achieved, is shown in Figure 1-5.

1-5 Black box diagram of Process

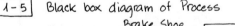
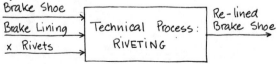

1 - 6 Technology

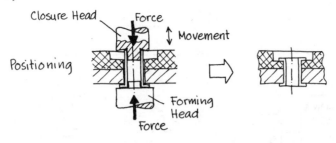

2.2 Establish the technological principles
Establish the sequence of operations

[The designer must now establish any technological principles that could bring about the transformations shown in the 'black box' diagram, select the most suitable principles, and if possible establish the optimum principle to satisfy the original problem statement and the design specification. One or more useful sequences of operations should be found, and the preferred one selected.

Any technology (i.e. the form of interaction between a technical system and a technical process – e.g. a tool, and the forming of a workpiece) that can be used is based on natural phenomena. The designer should therefore search all available knowledge and heuristics derived from experience and scientific endeavours, including the human and social sciences, crafts and manual skills, etc.]

In this case, a relatively simple technology already exists, not only in the form of a principle, but as an available set of operations. The technology described in Figure 1-6 is easier to understand than the black box representation, and has no sensible alternative. It is therefore regarded as the optimum.

2.3 Establish the technical processes,
TP → optimal TP

[The technical process (TP) now needs to be established in detail. This is achieved by establishing the operations required for the transformation of the operand, using the selected technology and sequence of operations, and attempting to balance advantages and disadvantages inherent in the possible technical processes.

An aid to complete this stage is the general model of the structure of technical processes (*Principles*, Figure 2) which shows the various categories of operation. The important parts of this structure for the current design step are:

(a) the 'preparation', 'execution' and 'conclusion' phases of transformation of the operand, and
(b) the partial processes for the operand, and supply of energy and information

See *Principles*, statement TP 4.]

Starting documents for this step are the black box diagram and the sketch of technology, Figures 1-5 and 1-6.

The technical process (TP: riveting) as represented (sketched and described by a model) in Figure 1-7 is likely to be optimal as there are no obvious alternatives. It encompasses the transformations of the operand, including all operations that are needed to realize the changes to the three operands to make them into one unified piece (starting state: separate items of brake shoe, lining, rivets; finishing state: riveted brake shoe). The necessary effects (*Principles*, Glossary definition 19) that have now been formulated in this figure can be applied to the process either by human operators or by technical systems (TS), as indicated in Figure 1-7. In addition, the preparation and conclusion phases for the processes of acquiring and using the TS must be considered: transportation, installation, replacement of parts, cleaning, etc.

2.4 Apply technical systems to the process, and establish boundaries

[In this step the designer has to establish the duties expected of the technical system (TS) from the requirements set by the technical process (TP), and distribute these duties between the various technical systems and sub-systems (especially if the TS is divided into a number of smaller units) and the human operators.

The necessary effects to be exerted on the technical process can be delivered to that TP either by a human being or by a technical system (TS) (see *Principles*, statement TP 5). Questions about the boundaries of the technical system, and possibly the number of participating technical systems, should also be considered at this stage.]

Starting from the TP, Figure 1-7, the duties of the TS need to be established (in addition to those required by the technological principle of riveting as shown in Figure 1-6). The probable number of separate TS needed to fulfil the duties is only one. The duties of the human operator are established as shown in Figure

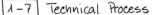

1-7 Technical Process

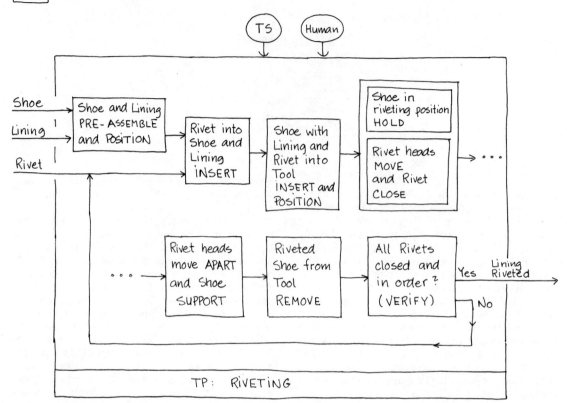

1-8. After considering the design specification, the designer decides that the tasks of the TS should comprise only moving the riveting heads and amplifying the input force.

2.5   Establish the grouping of functions

[The designer must now group the functions in useful ways. The choices can range from combining a number of functions to be performed by one function-carrier (organ, interaction location) to allocating them to a particular technical system (TS).

The term 'function' refers to the duty that the TS must be capable of performing (see *Principles*, Glossary definition 25). It is frequently possible to generate a number of different groupings of functions,

1-8 Functional structure of Operator

- Preparation of Tool
- Pre-assembly of Shoe and Lining
- Insertion of Rivet
- Positioning of Component in Tool
- Actuation of Tool
- Removal of Brake Shoe
- Removal of Tool

↓↓ Effects

e.g. deriving all the motions (and the energy) required from that TS from one, two, or more than two prime movers.]

In this simple problem this step could have been omitted from the procedural plan.

2.6 Establish the functional structures, and represent them

[The designer should now decide on the best functional structure with which to describe this problem. This includes representing by lists, sketches and models the decisions made up to now (see steps 2.4 and 2.5), and adding any other useful relationships.

The functions and their relationships are represented according to the guidelines of the general model of the functional structure (*Principles*, Figure 4). A feature of this procedure is that connections to each of the main transformation functions are established from the auxiliary functions, the propulsion functions, and the control and regulation functions (compare *Principles*, statement MS 2).

The form of wording used to define the functions in the functional structure can help to improve understanding of the problem, particularly by stressing actions and activities required from the machine or its operator:

● The effects exerted by the technical system are described by words showing an activity of one part of the technical system on another (e.g. 'riveting heads GUIDE') or on its environment. The TS is then described as 'active'.

● Where the human being (or other external agency) will perform operations within or in co-operation with the technical system, the function of the machine is to allow or accept the action applied from outside. The TS function is then expressed by words showing that the technical system must be ready to receive an effect (e.g. 'positioning of shoe and lining ENABLE'). The TS may then react, but until it receives an effect it is termed 'passive'.]

Starting from the TP (Figure 1-7) and the decisions in step 2.5, the functional structure that the designer has generated is shown in Figure 1-9. The process structure is very similar to the functional structure in this case study (compare Figures 1-6 and 1-7), but it should be noted that the form of representation used at this stage can vary (compare *Principles*, p. 52, step F).

It is, of course, possible to generate other ways of performing some of the functions in this functional structure, for instance:

Variant A If the circumstances warrant it, the function of positioning the brake shoes can be partially or totally allocated to the technical system, relieving the human being of that task.

Variant B The function 'Energy STORE' in this variant indicates that the riveting heads could be separated after the riveting operation by means of stored energy (e.g. by springs). This stored energy will be supplied by the force and motion which is supplied by the human operator to activate the tool.

Variant C The function 'Stability on the table ENSURE' can be performed by the tool itself (e.g. by means of a heavy base plate), or by an additional device (e.g. a vice, or screw clamps). In the latter case, the function could read 'Clamping to the table PERMIT'. In general, this function is better defined as 'Connection to a fixed system PERMIT', because this form of wording encourages a wider range of solutions.

2.7 Σ Functional structures
Improve Evaluate, decide Verify

[In this step, the first aim is to ensure that the previous work is properly collected and documented. This should be reviewed to check that it is complete, and to verify that the information is as correct as possible. The variants should be evaluated in two respects: to detect weak points that can be improved, and then to select the most favourable variants for processing in the next stages.]

Evaluation of these variants to the functional structure is best left to a later stage for this problem, as has been indicated in the procedural scheme, Figure 1-1.

Optimal functional structure

[A decision must be made on the most favourable functional structure, on which further progress towards hardware can be based.]

3 Aim: establish the concepts

[This sequence of steps is aimed at:

(a) establishing a set of abstract principles and organs for transferring effects from one TS (or part of a TS) to another and showing their relationships in the form of an organ structure,

(b) discovering or creating principles according to which the parts of a TS could possibly act (working principles), and abstract machine elements which can perform the TS functions (the function-carriers or organs), and

(c) showing relationships between function-carriers to form an outline of the technical system, an abstract anatomical structure or concept for the device (*Principles*, Glossary items 34 and 44).

The representation of this anatomical structure is largely without definition of form with the exception

1-9 Functional structure of the machine system

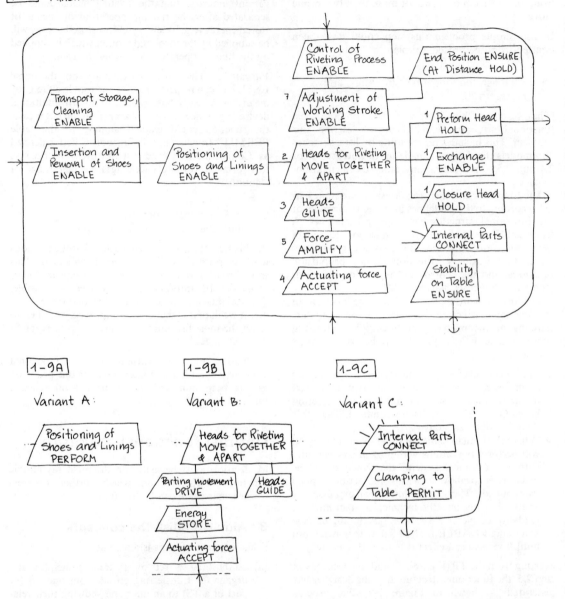

Variant A:

Positioning of Shoes and Linings PERFORM

Variant B:

Heads for Riveting MOVE TOGETHER & APART

Parting movement DRIVE

Heads GUIDE

Energy STORE

Actuating force ACCEPT

Variant C:

Internal Parts CONNECT

Clamping to Table PERMIT

---

of the necessary action locations or working surfaces, and as such it is typically a set of line diagrams with important surfaces shown in detail. The possible modes of action of the proposed machine must be considered. A viable total solution can usually be found by combining viable sub-solutions or partial systems (*Principles*, statement MS 3).]

3.1   Establish the inputs and modes of action

[This step encourages the designer to state or re-state the inputs to the TS, especially as they relate to and affect the possible modes of action of the machine. It is also useful to define the outputs from each stage, especially for a technical system consisting of a number of separable machine systems where the output of one TS can be the input to another.]

3.2   Establish the classes of function-carrier (morphological matrix)

[The designer must now find possible function-carriers (organs) for the TS functions, at this stage ignoring sizes and other details of construction. The

1-10 Morphological Matrix

Action Principles (AP) / Function-Carriers (FC)

#	Functions		Action Principles / Function-Carriers
1	Closure & Reform heads replaceably CONNECT and HOLD	AP	Single Head replaceable — Mechanical [Force-Locking, Form-Locking] · Magnetic · Pneumatic · Revolver Head
		FC	Screw head · Bayonet coupling · Cross coupling pin · Latch · Screw · Cone · Clamp · Gravity pin · Tension pin · Permanent · Electro · Pressure · Vacuum
2	Heads for Riveting MOVE TOGETHER and APART	AP	Linear Motion [Linear Input, Rotary Input] · Rotational [Linear Input, Rotary Input]
		FC	(symbols)
3	Heads GUIDE	AP	Linear [Sliding Guide, Rolling Guide, Elastic] · Rotational [Sliding Guide, Rolling Guide, Elastic]
		FC	Cylind. round · Polygon · Ball sleeve · Thomson Bearing · Coil spring · Rubber spring · Bronze Bearing · Needle Bearing · Ball Bearing · Roller Bearing · Leaf Spring
4	Actuating Force ACCEPT	AP	Rotary Movement [Foot, Hand] · Linear [Hand] · Impact Movement with Hammer or Guided Mass
		FC	Pedal · Stirrup · Lever Wheel · Push Rod · Pull Rod
5	Force AMPLIFY	AP	Mechanical · Hydraulic / Pneumatic · None
		FC	Lever [1 arm, 2 arms] · Eccentric Cam · Wedge · Screw Spindle · Rack & Pinion · Cable Link · Toggle Lever · Step Piston · Piston Ratio
6	End Position ENSURE (Heads for Riveting MOVE APART)	AP	Retracting Force from Energy Store — Mechanical [Springs, Weight, Massive, Torsion] · Hydro/Pneu. · from Hand Op. e.g. Lever, see ④
		FC	Helical · Leaf · Rod · Massive · Torsion · Bubble Chamber · Piston · Connect [Force-locking, Force-locking] · Latch · Friction · Self-locking Spindle
7	Adjustment of Working Stroke ENABLE	AP	Working Stroke long enough and Constant · Stroke limiting with Stop · Movement of Head Piece
		FC	Collar · Shim · Adjust Screw · Adjust Nut · Connected with Choice of Head · Change of Head Mechanism (stroke)
8	Positioning of Shoes and Lining ENABLE	AP	Suppression of individual Degrees of Freedom
		FC	(symbols)

▨ = Combination used in Fig. 1-13

search is for classes of function-carrier, rather than one specific answer to the problem.

Function-carriers are technical systems that are capable by virtue of their mode of action of performing required functions. Frequently a number of different modes of action (based on various natural phenomena) are available (*Principles*, statement MS 4), and therefore a number of different classes of function-carrier is available (*Principles*, statement MS 15).]

Starting from the functional structure, Figure 1-9, the morphological matrix resulting from this step is shown in Figure 1-10. The first column lists the functions required of the TS (with numbering as in

Figure 1-9). For each of these functions, the action principles, and suitable means of realizing the functions are stated at various levels of abstraction. The tabulation of the morphological matrix helps to maintain a sufficient overview of the design process to ensure that a coherent and possibly novel product emerges.

3.3   Combine the function-carriers, examine their relationships

[The designer now attempts to find potential solutions as combinations of the classes of function-carriers.

Every combination of function-carriers (e.g. the

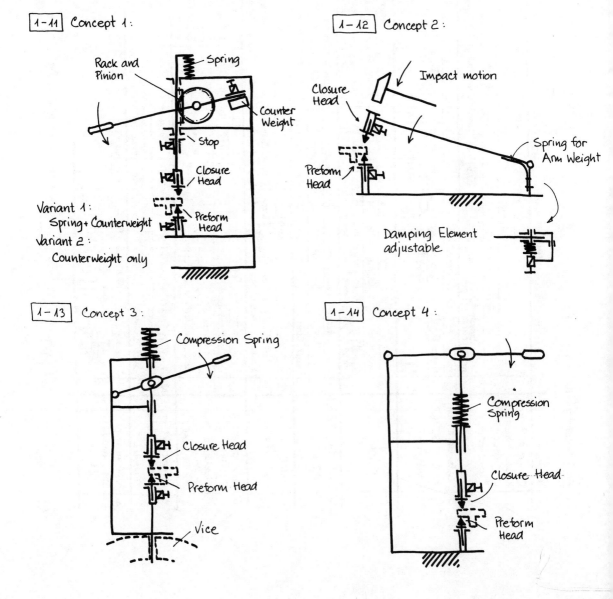

1-11 Concept 1:

1-12 Concept 2:

1-13 Concept 3:

1-14 Concept 4:

one marked in Figure 1-10) is potentially the basis for a concept and an anatomical structure. By formulating such combinations, the compatibility of the individual function-carrier can be tested, and problems involved in combining each one with the others can be assessed.]

3.4 Establish basic arrangement

[Starting from the partial function-carriers, or classes of them, the aim of this step is to evolve a number of concepts, and experiment with various basic arrangements.]

The designer's work on combining function-carriers has resulted in concept sketches, Figures 1-11 to 1-18. These are the results of a number of attempts to explore possible arrangements, and continual refinement until they seem satisfactory. The action of drawing these concepts may result in some poor ideas, which should not be allowed to become fixed. It is therefore necessary to represent these basic arrangements as principles only, with little or no detail.

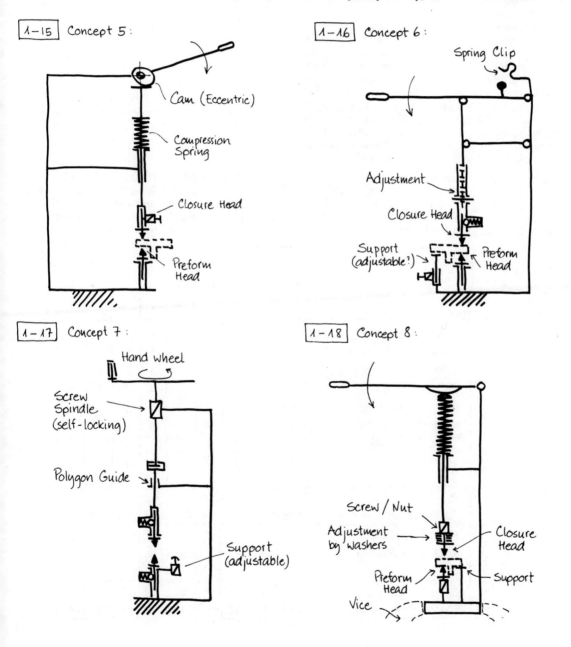

Every basic arrangement or combination of solutions can be varied in its spatial relationships. The problems of the relative positioning of the elements can be solved in different ways. The solutions shown here are only a sample of the possible combinations, but the solution space is adequately covered.

3.5 Σ Concepts
Improve   Evaluate, decide   Verify

[The aim here here is to establish the optimal concept, by checking, verifying, improving, evaluating and deciding, as outlined for step 2.7 above.

One possibility for evaluating these concepts is to use a points scoring assessment, the ideal solution being rated at 4 points (compare *Principles*, p. 69). An assessment for each solution is entered into the chart, the sum of the point-values is determined, and the relative proportion of the ideal score is calculated. These scores are then plotted on a 'relative strength diagram' (see *Principles*, p. 71). The solution with the highest rating is usually chosen, if this choice can be made with sufficient certainty. Otherwise, two or more solutions should be carried forward.]

The result of this evaluation is shown in Figures 1-19, 1-20, and yields an assessment showing a relatively high quality rating for all of the proposed solutions. The evaluation in this case does not show a large difference of ratings between concept principles 4, 5

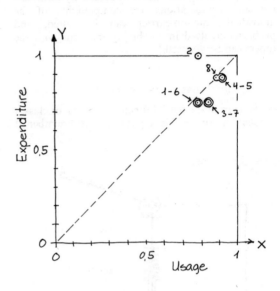

1-20   Relative Strength Diagram:

and 8 (Figures 1-14, 1-15 and 1-18), consequently three concepts are taken forward into the next stages. The designer now examines these concepts for possibilities of improving their weak areas, without necessarily searching for additional concepts.

1-19   Evaluation:

Concept Variant:

	Criteria:	1	2	3	4	5	6	7	8	Ideal
Usage Criteria	Speed of Riveting	4	4	4	4	4	4	2	4	4
	Quality of Riveting	4	3	4	4	4	3	4	4	4
	Stability and Time	3	3	4	4	4	3	3	4	4
	Operation Force	3	1	3	3	3	3	3	2	4
	Ease of Servicing	2	4	3	3	3	4	3	4	4
	Storage possibility	3	4	2	4	4	3	4	3	4
	Transportability	3	4	3	4	4	2	4	4	4
	Reliability	3	2	4	3	3	3	4	3	4
	Σ:	25	25	27	29	29	25	27	28	32
	Technical Rel. Value X:	0.78	0.78	0.84	0.91	0.91	0.78	0.84	0.88	1.00
Expenditure	No. of Parts	3	4	3	4	4	3	3	4	4
	Ease of Assembly	3	4	3	3	3	3	3	3	4
	Σ:	6	8	6	7	7	6	6	7	8
	Economic Rel. Value Y:	0.75	1	0.75	0.88	0.88	0.75	0.75	0.88	1.00

Optimal concept

[Ideally, this event is reached by deciding on one concept judged to be the best under the circumstances: the optimum (based on the state of the art, the design specification, and the previous work).]

4 Aim: establish the preliminary layouts

[This sequence of steps encompasses establishing a first rough layout of the anatomical structure of the technical system. It usually takes the form of sketches and rough arrangement drawings, with descriptions of the most important constructional elements (i.e. their roughly defined form, dimensions and manufacturing methods). In particular, their arrangement relative to one another must be considered. This stage generally proceeds in six steps, as follows.]

4.1   Establish the orientation points for form determination

[The designer now aims to establish the starting position for determining form. Important aids in this step are sketches, roughly to scale, using orthogonal or pictorial views.

Additional information needs to be found in tables of ergonomic data, and simple experiments conducted on wooden or cardboard models to simulate insertion of the brake shoes and operation of the equipment.]

In addition to the accepted concepts, Figures 1-14, 1-15 and 1-18, the following information helps to provide a starting point:

● Working stroke and free travel of the riveting heads.
● Clearance for possible positioning of the brake shoes in the riveting space (see Figure 1-21).
● Generation and transmission of the riveting forces, starting from the operator's input. Approximate size determination for the mechanism.

● Spatial arrangement of the operating station, including height and accessibility of the riveting space, and actuation of the mechanism (see Figure 1-21).

4.2   Establish the arrangement, investigate re-use, rough form-giving, partial dimensioning

[This step instructs the designer to consider the geometry of the components and their relationships to each other, establishing dimensions only where this is necessary for establishing the arrangement. Possibilities of re-use of parts or systems that were designed in the past for other duties should also be considered:

(a) by searching for appropriate components in the drawings of other equipment, assessing bought-out components and machine elements, or considering standard parts,
(b) by reviewing all the outputs of the proposed system, especially those material and energy outputs that are not the primary products of the transformation, and considering re-cycling or potential sales of these secondary products.]

In this case, one aspect of these considerations is covered in a comment in step 4.4.

4.3   Establish the types of material, classes of manufacturing method, tolerances and surface properties where necessary

[The aim in this step is to make decisions regarding the form for the TS. Form determination, whether rough and preliminary or detailed and definitive, requires that the designer establishes a number of design properties (*Principles*, Glossary definition 16) according to the model of progressive generation of information (*Principles*, Figure 11). The definitive arrangement, form, dimensions, materials, etc. must be established and recorded. These properties of the technical system also show mutual interrelationships.

1-21   Basis for Form Determination:

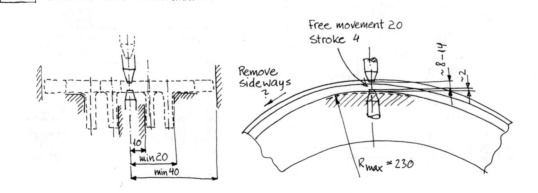

It is therefore usually necessary to proceed through several iterations within this phase, e.g.

(a) initial assumptions, for instance of some approximate dimensions;

(b) rough calculations based on (a), particularly using those quantities that determine the basic sizes, for instance the strength or rigidity of the selected material,

(c) with these revised quantities or dimensions used as the new initial assumption, the iteration is repeated as outlined in (b).

The results of these verifications of strength (or other calculated properties of the technical system) allow the designer to decide whether to accept the revised quantity, or whether it is necessary to proceed through another iteration.]

This riveting tool is so simple that a further iteration to refine the ideas is not needed, and rough form-determination can proceed in a single cycle. The following steps include a number of attempts to explore the situation, and various refinements leading to the final accepted versions.

4.4   Investigate the critical form-determination zones

[The aim in this step is to investigate difficult or problematical regions of the proposed TS with respect to their form, and to generate variants.]

This simple TS, the riveting tool, does not require any particular investigations of such critical regions, with the possible exception of the geometry of the rivet closure head, if it is to be designed as part of the TS. Alternatively, this item may be obtained by 're-use' (see step 4.2 for explanation): by using a bought-out component, an item in the existing manufacturing programme, or a part for which a drawing exists. This decision is deferred to the detail design phase.

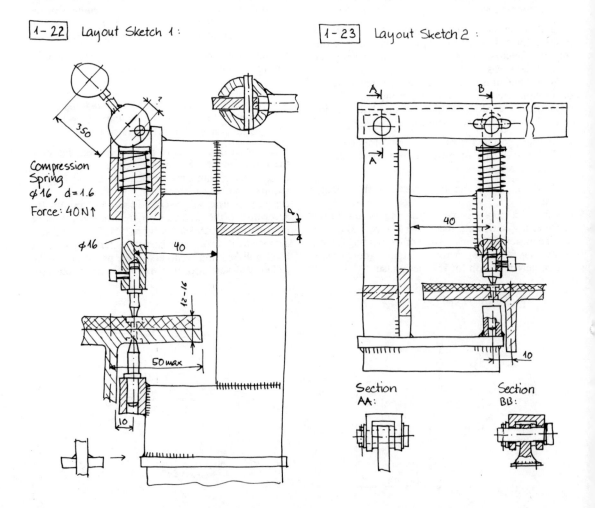

1-22 Layout Sketch 1:

1-23 Layout Sketch 2:

4.5 Represent the preliminary layouts

[The designer should now aim to represent the technical system as the carrier of all properties that have been established in the preceding steps.]

The result of work in this step is a set of preliminary layouts in good sketch form, Figures 1-22 to 1-24. These layouts, roughly to scale, are a continuation of making the concept sketches more concrete. A number of variants can be generated from each concept, by appropriate variations of the design characteristics. This is not demonstrated here, because this example is intended to emphasise the stages of concept-formation.

4.6 Σ Preliminary layout
Improve   Evaluate, decide   Verify

[The designer should now select the optimal variant(s) based on verification, improvement, and an evaluation.]

The final selection for this example will take place in the next phase, because by then better and more concrete data will be available. Only variant 2 is eliminated in this step as it is clearly inferior. This decision is verified by the subsequent evaluation, performed in step 5.6, and shown in Figure 1-27.

Optimum preliminary layout

[The result of design work leading up to this event is ideally a single preliminary layout, probably in sketch form and roughly to scale.]

5 Aim: establish the dimensional layouts

[The purpose of this sequence of steps is to establish the final anatomical structure, which includes fairly accurate descriptions of all constructional elements.]

In this relatively simple case, the designer decides to combine this sequence of steps into a single operation which consists of attempts to formulate solutions to the immediate problems, followed by refinement to reach an acceptable set of solutions.

1-24 | Layout Sketch 3 :

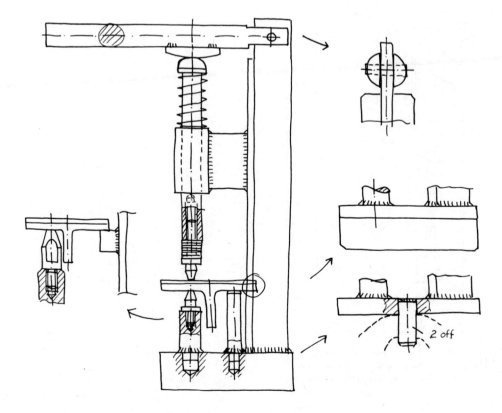

2 off

5.1   Deliver the substantiation for certain design characteristics

[The designer should now perform any necessary calculations (for strengths, flow rates, friction losses, etc.) that have not been done for the previous steps, and should review and justify the choices that led up to the dimensional layout (in addition to those that were considered in step 3.5), by referring to the design specification.]

5.2   Establish the definitive arrangement, form determination, partial dimensioning

[The designer should consider each component, decide on the final arrangements and geometries, and establish the most important dimensions, and any other critical sizes or quantities.]

5.3   Establish the definitive and complete determination of materials, manufacturing methods, partial definitive determination of tolerances and surface properties

[In this step, the considerations needed to prepare for detail drawing of the most important functional components should be completed, including choice of materials, surface treatments, tolerances, etc.]

5.4   Optimize the critical form determination zones

[This step repeats all considerations of the preliminary layout stage, but at a more concrete level. The explanations given in phase 4, particularly step 4.4, refer equally to this phase.]

| 1-25 | Dimensional Layout 1 :

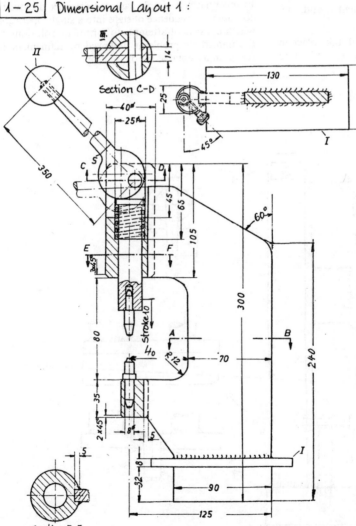

1-26 Dimensional Layout 2:

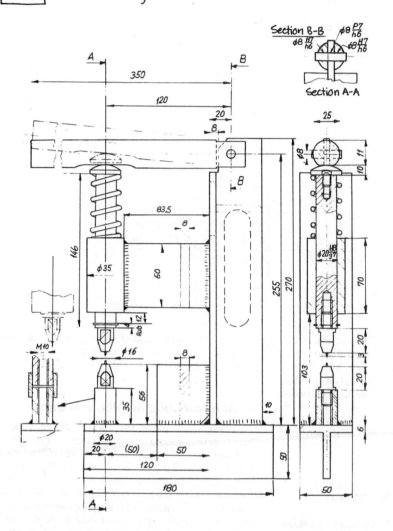

Section B-B $\phi 8 \frac{P7}{h6}$
$\phi 8 \frac{H7}{h6}$ $\phi 8 \frac{H7}{h6}$

Section A-A

An additional consideration in this dimensional layout stage consists of investigating any transverse forces, friction forces, moments, clearances, possibilities of jamming in the guideways, and resultant positional accuracies of the riveting heads.

5.5   Represent the dimensional layouts

[This task asks the designer to draw and describe the TS as the means of achieving the previously established design characteristics, i.e. the technical means of achieving the functions and effects to be exerted by the TS on the TP.]

This work is described in the dimensional layouts, Figures 1-25 and 1-26. The execution of these layouts consists not only of making the design results more concrete, but also of various changes to other design characteristics. For instance, the first of these layouts, Figure 1-25, shows the frame flame-cut from a piece of plate instead of a welded fabrication, because the parts are relatively small. These variations of basic arrangement and form are transferable between the layouts and may need to be separately evaluated with respect to each layout. Other alternatives and their comparisons are left to the reader.

5.6   Σ Dimensional layout
   Improve   Evaluate, decide   Verify

[The designer must now select the optimum solution from the variants developed earlier, considering all the criteria contained in the design specification, other documents, estimates of costs, etc. Weak points should, if necessary, be improved.]

1-27   Evaluation of dimensional Layouts:

	Criteria:	Lay-outs: 1	2	3	Ideal
Usage Criteria	Speed of Riveting	3	3	3	4
	Quality of Riveting	3	3	3	4
	Stability and time	3	3	4	4
	Operation, Force	3	2	3	4
	Ease of Servicing	3	3	4	4
	Storage possibility	3	3	3	4
	Transportability	3	2	2	4
	Reliability	3	4	4	4
	Appearance	4	2	3	4
	Σ :	28	25	29	36
	Techn. Rel. Value X	0.78	0.69	0.80	1.00
Expend.	Manufacturing Cost ~	350 Fr.	290 Fr.	280 Fr.	
	Detailing Costs ~	4	3	3	

The designer's results are in the evaluation table, Figure 1-27, and the dimensional layout, Figure 1-26. The evaluation has established variant 3 as the one best suited to this set of circumstances. Details of this procedure are not discussed here. The weakest point, as judged by this evaluation and shown in the chart, is transportability. One possibility for improving this aspect is indicated in the dashed lines of a hand-hold cut into the frame (Figure 1-26).

Optimal dimensional layout

[This event is characterised by the existence of a single dimensional layout that has been chosen as optimal for the solution of this problem.]

Concluding steps 6.1 to 6.7 are not developed for this case, but descriptions of these steps follow.

Release for detailing

[It is normal practice to review the design work up to this stage, before permitting further work. If it is decided that the project should continue, a general freeze on layout changes is usually imposed.

Up to this point, some money has been expended to investigate the problem and propose a solution. The cost of work increases rapidly in the following detailing stages. Estimates of manufacturing and

running costs on the basis of existing information can be quite good. A firm economic decision on continuing the project should now be taken.]

6 Aim: produce details, elaborate

[This last sequence in the formal design process (before development work starts) aims to provide all necessary information for manufacture (at least for a prototype, if a larger number of the TS is to be manufactured), testing, maintenance, servicing, operation, safety procedures, etc. Full records are also assembled to document the design decisions, permit review and second generation improvements, and provide the necessary product information to other sections of the company, e.g. sales and marketing, service and maintenance/repair, etc.]

6.1   Deliver the substantiation for detail decisions

6.2   Establish the final forms, definitive and complete dimensioning

6.3   Establish the definitive and complete materials, manufacturing methods, tolerances, surface properties

6.4   Establish the assembly procedures and intermediate states of assembly

6.5   Represent the parts, dimensions, tolerances, surface properties, material specifications

6.6   Produce the assembly drawings, parts lists, and prepare further documents

6.7   Σ Documentation for manufacture
Improve   Evaluate, decide   Verify

[At some stage in this process of detailing, a freeze on all design changes is usually imposed, to avoid extra costs from changes to parts that have already been manufactured or ordered. If the technical system is now manufactured as a prototype, an opportunity to change and incorporate improvements exists in the next cycle of 're-design and review' (following the same systematic design procedure as used here), before the TS is manufactured for sale. If this TS is to be manufactured as a single item or batch with little prospect of repeat orders, the first product of the batch can act as prototype, or the prototype is later commissioned as the finished TS.]

This TS is basically intended as a one-off item, and all its parts will be made at one time. If sales are anticipated, changes can be made between the 'in-house' series and the 'for sale' series.

Representation of complete technical system

[All necessary documents and information now exist for manufacture and operation. If this device is to be placed on the market, the sales and marketing departments can now prepare for the launch of the product, with adequate knowledge of expected system properties (subject to prototype testing and development), including cost estimates.]

Case 2 Milling fixture

A milling fixture, a simple technical system, serves as the second design study. The procedure is illustrated in Figure 2-1, based on the general plans of Figures 0-1 and 0-2, and gives a clear survey of the design documents generated during design work on this problem. The emphasis is again on the phase of concept creation.

Introduction

A mechanical engineering manufacturer produces large quantities of a slotted pin shown in Figure 2-2. Milling the 6 mm wide slot without a special fixture to hold the pins is expensive, and does not permit full use of the milling machine. The task of designing a suitable milling fixture is assigned to a designer in the jig and tool department. The problem assignment includes the drawing of the pin, and details of annual manufacturing quantities.

Problem assignment

1 Aim: elaborate or clarify the assigned specifications

1.1 Critically recognize the assigned problem

1.2 Establish the state of the art

1.3 Analyse the problem situation

1.4 Examine the possibilities of realization

Steps 1.1 to 1.4 are omitted for this case.

For an experienced designer of jigs and tools, this task is sufficiently routine that detailed analyses or investigations are not needed at this stage. The designer is familiar with the practice in this relatively narrow specialization of jig and tool design, has good knowledge of the whole range of equipment in the manufacturing plant, and has on file the outline drawings, capacity charts and other data for each machine tool.

[Only a few further preparatory studies are needed in this case; the designer can proceed almost directly to preparing the list of requirements. Nevertheless, it would be wrong to omit the step of setting up a design

specification with the excuse that 'this task is a well-known repeat job'. Systematic design must follow the basic rule that a design specification (list of requirements) must be generated for each task (the arguments for this statement may be found in *Principles*). The designer may also consider it an advantage to have a 'contract' with management, by asking for a signature on this design specification to indicate management agreement with its contents. In order to save time, pre-printed forms should be used for this purpose, and such forms can be generated in great detail for a relatively specialized area such as machine tool fixtures.]

1.5 Complete the requirements, classify and quantify, set priorities

1.6 Work out the full design specification (list of requirements)

Comments refer to combined use of steps 1.5 and 1.6.

[Pre-printed forms for design specifications can be a great help in performing this step: a number of different forms can be generated to assist with distinct classes of tasks that are common in a particular design office.]

The result of the designer's early efforts on the project is the design specification in Figure 2-3, which lists a number of categories to aid the designer's further work.

[A noteworthy feature of the specification in this example is the attempt to identify all elements of the technical system.]

1.7 Prepare and plan for problem-solving

[In this case, because the object to be designed is simple (low system complexity and low difficulty for the designer) the whole process as laid down in the model, Figure 0-1, is not necessary. All the steps are nevertheless retained as listed, to emphasize the generality of the design method.]

The emphasis in this design task is on establishing the mode of action for the solution. A timetable is proposed and is shown in Figure 2-4. A special procedural plan is not considered necessary.

Figure 2-1

Steps from General Model according to Figure 0.1	Step	Progress of case	Design documents
1 Aim: elaborate or clarify the assigned specification	1.1 1.2 1.3 1.4 1.5 1.6 1.7	Problem Assignment 2-2 → 2-3 2-4	Design Specification Timetable
2 Aim: establish the functional structures	2.1 2.2 2.3 2.4 2.5 2.6 2.7	2-5 2-6 2-7 2-8 2-9 2-10	Black Box Diagram Techn. Process Diagram Technological Principles Functional Structure (Hierarchial Tree)
3 Aim: establish the concepts	3.1 3.2 3.3 3.4 3.5	2-11 2-12 2-13 2-14 2-15 2-16 2-17 2-18	Morphological Matrix Concepts Evaluation Chart "Ideal Solutions" Optimum Concept
4 Aim: establish the preliminary layouts	4.1 4.2 4.3 4.4 4.5 4.6	2-19 2-12 2-14 2-20 2-21	Sketches for rough Form Determination
5 Aim: establish the dimensional layouts	5.1 5.2 5.3 5.4 5.5 5.6	2-22 2-23 2-24 2-25	Dimensional Layouts Evaluation Chart
6 Aim: detailing, elaboration	6.1 6.2 6.3 6.4 6.5 6.6 6.7	Release	

2-2 Problem assignment:

Design of a clamping fixture to assist milling of the slot in the pin as shown:

General tolerances: ± 0.3
Material: St 50-2
Manufacturing quantity:
                        10.000 per year.

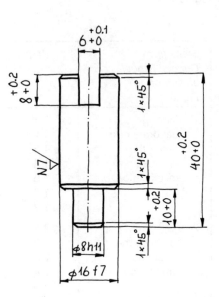

Design specification

2 Establish the functional structures

2.1 Abstract: produce the black box representation

[Experience shows that it is useful to extend the limits of the Technical Process (TP) where possible. This should yield a more complete understanding and a more comprehensive statement of the requirements for the technical system (TS).]

Figure 2-5 shows two processes described by 'black box' models. It is obvious that the process 'Pin HOLD' is a necessary part of the process 'Pin MILL'. In the light of the theoretical comment above, this case will therefore investigate the more complex TP: 'Pin MILL'.

2.2 Establish the technological principles
Establish the sequence of operations

The proposed sequence of operations is shown in Figure 2-6. The technology described in Figure 2-7 is in general use and is well known. It is therefore not likely to be subject to any unusual problems. Alternative technologies exist, but are not likely to be as productive. For this reason, the selected technology is regarded as optimal.

2.3 Establish the technical processes,
      TP → optimal TP

The starting documents for this step are shown in Figures 2-5, 2-6, 2-7. The TP as generated by the designer and represented in Figure 2-8 is regarded as optimal. It contains a complete description of the effects (*Principles*, Glossary item 19) needed to change the state of the operand (the pin). These effects must be brought about by the human operator or by the machine system.

[The operand is that part of the transformation system that is being worked upon and transformed. The operators, consisting of human beings, technical systems and the active environment, act upon the operand (fulfil their functions) by exerting certain effects. This convention is similar to the one usually defined for mathematical expressions.]

A secondary sequence at the foot of Figure 2-8 shows the preparation and conclusion phases for the TS: cleaning, positioning, etc.

2.4 Apply technical systems to the process, and establish boundaries

To ensure that the functional structure is not too abstract (which could occur in this problem if it is derived only from the TP) the designer can now start to analyse the important operations and to formulate the effects that the TS must cause at a more concrete level. It is clear that further decisions must be made. In this case, the important operations are 'positioning', 'clamping/releasing' and 'hold clamped'. This analysis is represented in Figure 2-9 together with the resultant partial functions.
  The duties of the TS need to be established and it is likely that a single TS will do all that is required. The duties of the human operator are established as

2-3

Design Specification		PROJECT:	Fixed Req.	Desire
WDK	Sheet 1/2	Milling Fixture		

1. Functions
    Clamping of Pin for milling   ×
    Rigid Mounting on machine table   ×
    Certainty of Positioning   ×

2. Conditions of the technical process
    2.1 Pin : from sketch (form, sizes)
        Material : St 50-2
        Cleaned and de-greased
        Mass : × [g]

    2.2 Environment :
        Milling Machine : Universal type UF 30
        Table feed motions 500 × 200 mm
        Spindle height above table 300 mm
        T-slots : Standard
        Cutting speed for this use: n r.p.m.
        Power : X [kW]
        Slotting Cutter : width 6 mm, diameter 80-100 mm
        Quality : Carbide tipped
        Coolant : type, quality, temperature
        Coolant removal   ×

    2.3 Clamping :
        Clamp force : S [N]
        Easy insertion and removal   ×

    2.4 Milling Process :
        Feed rate : v [m/s], No. of passes : A   ×
        Milling forces : V [N], H [N]   ×
        Loading / Unloading : manual   ×
        Arrangement : in line / parallel ?
        Chips must not stay in cutting region   ×

2-3 Continued :

Design Specification		PROJECT: Milling Fixture	Fixed Req.	Desire
WDK	Sheet 2/2			
3. Operation Properties				
Reliability			×	
Life : 2 years (with required precision)			×	
Easy mounting on milling table			×	
Easy Cleaning			×	
Easy Servicing				×
4. Ergonomic Properties				
Max. Force capability of operator : 200 N			×	
Safety of operator			×	
5. Appearance				
No particular requirements				
6. Distribution Properties				
Smallest possible storage space				×
7. Delivery Properties				
Delivery deadline : 3 months			×	
Design : 3 weeks			×	
8. Manufacturing Properties				
Machine tools available in this compagny			×	
9. Costs				
2000 SFr (materials and labour)			×	
Design costs not specified .				

2-4 Timetable:

Activity:	Hours:	Time Gantt Chart:
1. Problem Definition, Design Spec.	2 hrs.	
2. Functional structure	4 -	
3. Establishing Concepts	4 -	
4. Layouts, Decisions, Release	10 -	
5. Detailing, Documentation	20 -	
Total:	40 hrs.	

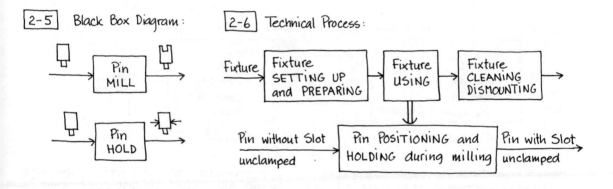

2-5 Black Box Diagram: 2-6 Technical Process:

2-7 Duty and technological Principle:

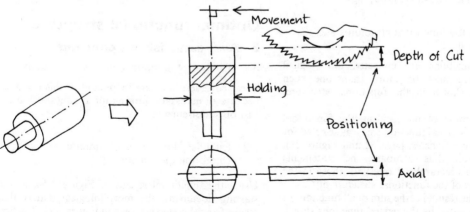

2-8 Detailed technical Process:

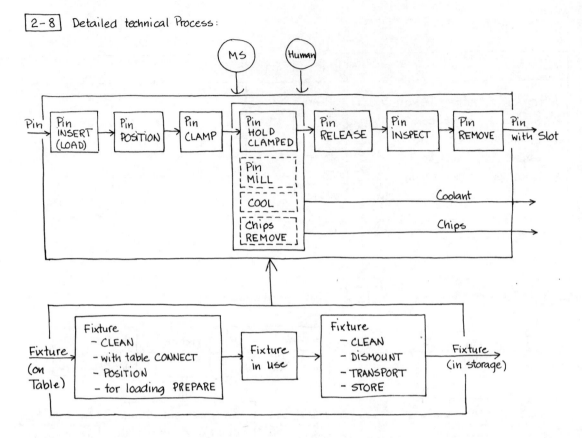

shown in Figure 2-10B. The designer decides which of the forces for clamping are to be delivered by the human operator, and not by the TS.

2.5 Establish the grouping of functions

In this problem, it is not necessary to collect any of the functions into more complex groupings.

2.6 Establish the functional structures and represent them

The partial functions are collected into logical sequences (there may be more than one such sequence) and shown in the functional structure, Figure 2-10A.

[For the purpose of representing the functional structure, a hierarchical function tree was selected for Figure 2-10 (see *Principles*, page 52 and Figure 21). The reader can thus compare the statements contained in this hierarchical tree with those in the block schematic of the functional structure of Case 1 (Figure 1-9). The result, i.e. the sum of all functions of the TS, is formulated by the partial functions shown at the ends of each branch of Figure 2-10A. It must be emphasized that the detail generated in this example

is only possible and useful for an experienced designer. Alternatives in the functional structure do not need to be investigated here.]

2.7 Σ Functional structures
Improve   Evaluate, decide   Verify

Optimal functional structure

3 Aim: establish the concepts

3.1 Establish the inputs and modes of action

These considerations are redundant in this example, because all necessary information is contained in the List of Requirements.

3.2 Establish the classes of function-carrier (morphological matrix)

Using the functional structure, Figure 2-10, as the starting document, the morphological matrix that results from this step is shown in Figure 2-11. The first column lists the functions (using the numbering in Figure 2-10), and for each of these the relevant action

2-9   Establish Functions:

A: Positioning:

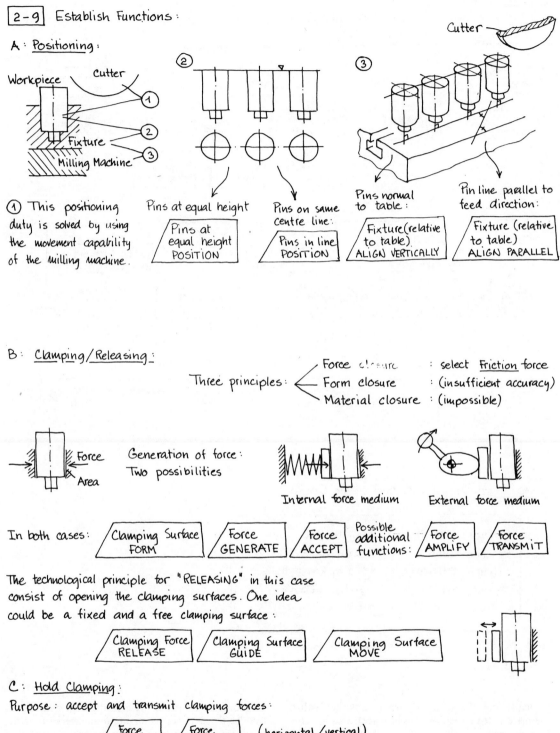

① This positioning duty is solved by using the movement capability of the milling machine.

Pins at equal height
> Pins at equal height POSITION

Pins on same centre line:
> Pins in line POSITION

Pins normal to table:
> Fixture(relative to table) ALIGN VERTICALLY

Pin line parallel to feed direction:
> Fixture (relative to table) ALIGN PARALLEL

B: Clamping/Releasing:

Three principles:
- Force closure : select **Friction** force
- Form closure : (insufficient accuracy)
- Material closure : (impossible)

Force
Area

Generation of force: Two possibilities

Internal force medium   External force medium

In both cases:
> Clamping Surface FORM

> Force GENERATE

> Force ACCEPT

Possible additional functions:
> Force AMPLIFY

> Force TRANSMIT

The technological principle for "RELEASING" in this case consist of opening the clamping surfaces. One idea could be a fixed and a free clamping surface:

> Clamping Force RELEASE

> Clamping Surface GUIDE

> Clamping Surface MOVE

C: Hold Clamping:

Purpose: accept and transmit clamping forces:

> Force ACCEPT

> Force TRANSMIT

(horizontal/vertical)

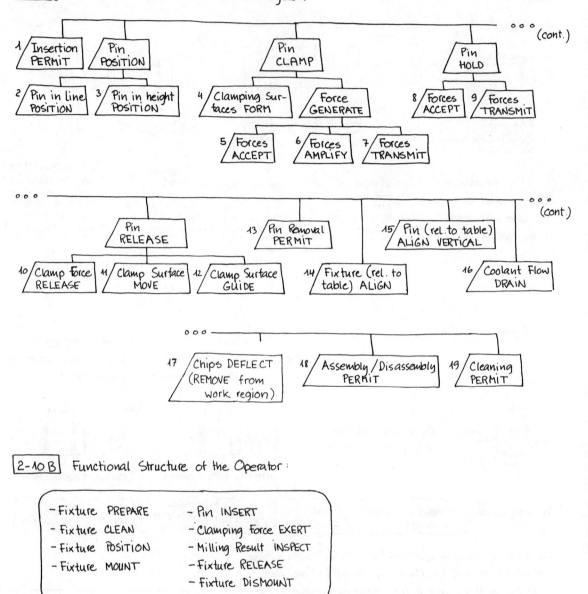

2-10A Functional Structure of the Machine System:

o o o (cont.)

1 / Insertion PERMIT
  Pin / POSITION
2 / Pin in line POSITION   3 / Pin in height POSITION
  Pin / CLAMP
4 / Clamping Surfaces FORM   Force / GENERATE
  Pin / HOLD
8 / Forces ACCEPT   9 / Forces TRANSMIT
5 / Forces ACCEPT   6 / Forces AMPLIFY   7 / Forces TRANSMIT

o o o   o o o (cont.)

  Pin / RELEASE
13 / Pin Removal PERMIT
15 / Pin (rel. to table) ALIGN VERTICAL
10 / Clamp Force RELEASE   11 / Clamp Surface MOVE   12 / Clamp Surface GUIDE
14 / Fixture (rel. to table) ALIGN
16 / Coolant Flow DRAIN

o o o
17 / Chips DEFLECT (REMOVE from work region)
18 / Assembly / Disassembly PERMIT
19 / Cleaning PERMIT

2-10 B Functional Structure of the Operator:

- Fixture PREPARE   - Pin INSERT
- Fixture CLEAN   - Clamping Force EXERT
- Fixture POSITION   - Milling Result INSPECT
- Fixture MOUNT   - Fixture RELEASE
                            - Fixture DISMOUNT

↓ ↓ Effects on MS

principle and the function-carriers able to realize them are stated (at various levels of abstraction). This is potentially a very creative phase, and prior knowledge of existing systems should be brought to bear. All the techniques of brainstorming (such as inverting the problem) will help to produce many solutions to the problems identified. In addition, it enables the designer to maintain an overview of the available alternatives since some may be capable of being more readily combined with solutions to other problems. Thus it helps towards an overall optimum solution.

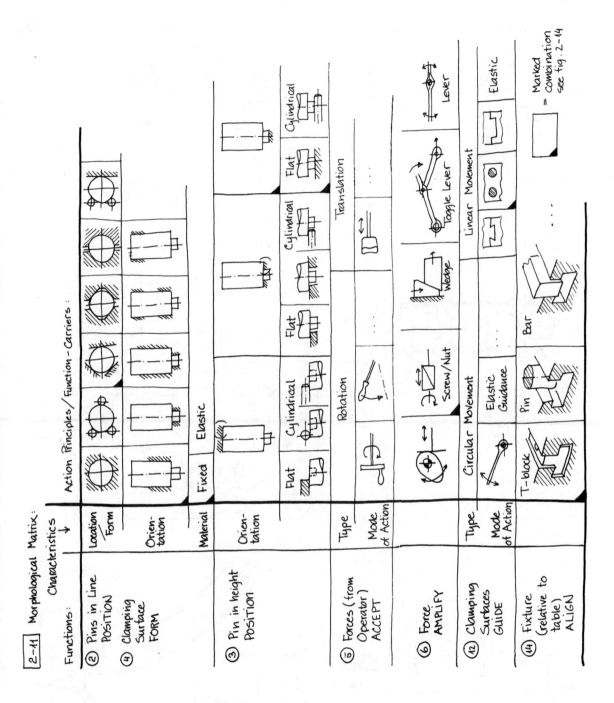

2-11 Morphological Matrix:

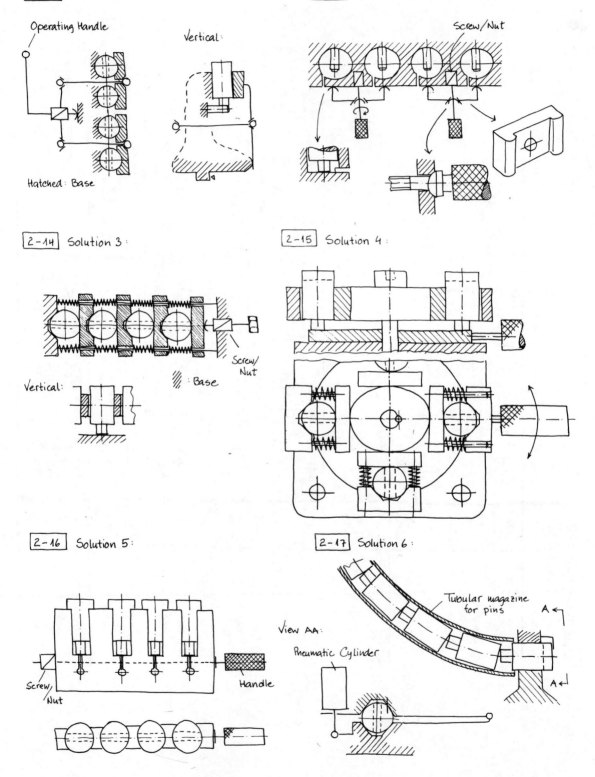

2-12 Solution 1:

Operating Handle

Vertical:

Hatched: Base

2-13 Solution 2:

Screw/Nut

2-14 Solution 3:

Screw/Nut

Vertical:

⊘: Base

2-15 Solution 4:

2-16 Solution 5:

Screw/Nut

Handle

2-17 Solution 6

Tubular magazine for pins

A

View AA:

Pneumatic Cylinder

A

3.3 Combine the function-carriers, examine their relationships

Each function-carrier is assessed for its compatibility with others, and to explore which combinations are easiest to realize.

3.4 Establish the basic arrangements

This step results in the concept sketches, Figures 2-12 to 2-17. The range of possibilities in the solutions shown here is relatively large, and demonstrates that an interesting variety of solutions can be generated from even a limited set of function-carriers, by varying their arrangements. It is typical of this development process of solutions that they are not uniform in their values. They do not fulfil all design requirements equally, and the detail shown in the solution proposals varies.

3.5 Σ Concepts
Improve   Evaluate, decide   Verify

This evaluation, shown in Figure 2-18, is based on only three usage criteria and two expenditure criteria. The ideal score has been chosen as 3. The evaluation is therefore coarse but easy to perform. A notional 'ideal solution' has been outlined in Figure 2-19.

Alternatives 1 and 3 emerge as best (by a small margin) from this evaluation, and are the only solutions to be taken further in this case description. The designer considers that a 'relative strength diagram' would not add useful information.

Optimal concept

4 Aim: establish the preliminary layouts

4.1 Establish the orientation points for form determination

The starting points for form determination in this case are the clamping points that are clearly shown in each variant. The material is then built up around these proposed concepts.

| 2-18 | Evaluation : |

	1	2	3	4	5	6	Ideal
Good use of force *	2	2	3	1	1	1	3
Reliability	3	3	2	2	1	1	3
High Productivity	3	3	3	3	3	1	3
Σ	8	8	8	6	5	3	9
Simplicity : few parts	3	2	3	1	1	1	3
Simplicity : simple forms	2	2	2	1	3	1	3
Σ	5	4	5	2	4	2	6

* Effective transfer of available hand force/torque to clamping force on workpiece.

| 2-19 | "Ideal" solutions : |

Cleaning :

Force direction :

Insertion :

Removal :
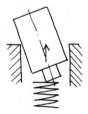

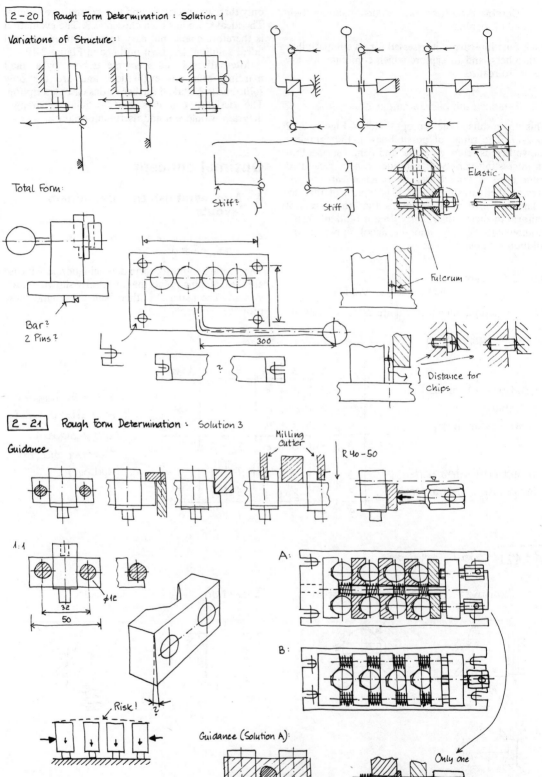

2-20   Rough Form Determination : Solution 1

Variations of Structure:

Total Form:

Stiff?

Stiff

Elastic

Fulcrum

Bar?
2 Pins?

300

Distance for chips

2-21   Rough Form Determination :   Solution 3

Guidance

Milling Cutter

R 40-50

1:1

32

ø12

50

Risk!

A:

B:

Only one

Guidance (Solution A):

2-22 Dimensional Layout : Solution 1

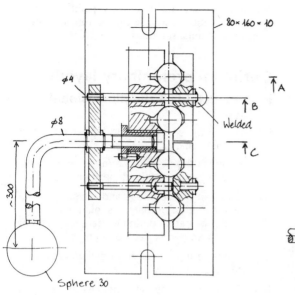

$80 \times 160 \times 10$

$\phi 4$

$\phi 8$

~300

Sphere 30

Welded

↑A

↑B

↑C

Section A:

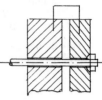

$\phi 6$

Section B:

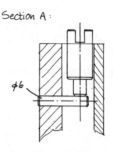

Section C:

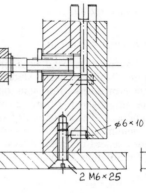

$2 \ M6 \times 25$

$\phi 6 \times 10$

Improvements:

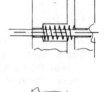

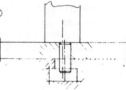

2-23 Dimensional Layout : Solution 3

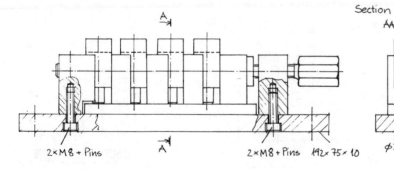

A

A

$2 \times M8 + Pins$

$2 \times M8 + Pins$ $192 \times 75 \times 10$

Section
AA:

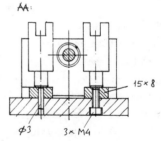

15×8

$\phi 3$ $3 \times M4$

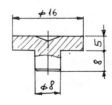

$\phi 16$

5

8

$\phi 8$

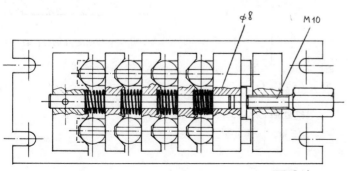

$\phi 8$ M10

4.2   Establish the arrangements, investigate re-use, rough form-giving, partial dimensioning

4.3   Establish the types of material, classes of manufacturing methods, tolerances and surface properties where necessary

This fixture is so simple that rough form determination needs only a single cycle.

4.4   Investigate critical form determination zones

This milling fixture shows no serious form determination problems, and special investigations are not needed.

Steps 4.2 to 4.4 are omitted for this case.

4.5   Represent the preliminary layouts

Work on this step has produced the preliminary sketch layouts, Figures 2-20 and 2-21, which still contain many abstract members. For solution 1, several variants are investigated before a more concrete sketch is produced. The execution of these sketches shows a minimum of detail, which is only permissible for an experienced designer. A two-row variant is developed for Solution 2, which may result in higher productivity.

4.6   Σ Preliminary layout
       Improve   Evaluate, decide   Verify

No decisions are taken at this point about the optimum solution. Two are carried forward into dimensional layouts: solutions 1 and 3A.

Optimum preliminary layout

5   Aim: establish the dimensional layout

5.1   Deliver the substantiation for certain design characteristics

5.2   Establish the definitive arrangement, form determination, partial dimensioning

5.3   Establish the definitive and complete determination of materials, manufacturing methods, partial definitive determination of tolerances and surface properties

5.4   Optimize the critical form determination zones

5.5   Represent the dimensional layouts

Comments refer to combined use of steps 5.1 to 5.5.

Dimensional layouts produced by the designer are shown in Figures 2-22 and 2-23. The appearance of

2-24 Evaluation:

Solution	1	3A	Ideal
Rigid clamping	2	3	3
Certain Positioning	3	2	3
Comfortable Operation	2	2	3
Good use of Force (see fig 2-18)	2	3	3
Low Chip Sensitivity	3	2	3
Productivity (Weight 2×)	4	6	6
User Value : Σ	16	18	21
	(0,8)	(0,9)	
Manufacturing Costs	2	2	3
Detailing Costs	2	2	3
Economic Rel. Value Σ	4	4	6
	(0,6)	(0,6)	
Manufacturing Cost Estimate	1200 SFr	1300 SFr	
Detailing Cost Estimate (time)	15 hrs.	15 hrs.	

2-25 Improvements:

Supporting bar

Elastic Material

these two layouts indicates that this is the work of an experienced design engineer who does not need to spend much time and effort on details of form, particularly since he will prepare his own detail drawings, as is usual in jig and tool design.

5.6 Σ Dimensional layout
Improve   Evaluate, decide   Verify

The evaluation produced by the designer (Figure 2-24) reveals that solution 3 can be improved by adding a top clamp, and setting the pin ends on elastic pads (Figure 2-25). This solution is better, particularly with respect to the usage criteria. The number of criteria has been expanded. Allocation of point values is still a difficult procedure that cannot really be regarded as objective. Any errors or misunderstandings in this evaluation could have serious repercussions, as the numbers evolved may cloud overall engineering judgement.

Concluding steps 6.1 to 6.7 are not developed for this case.

Case 3 Powder-coating machine

This foodstuff coating machine is a complex technical system. The design process comprises not only the design of the final, total machine, but also that of some sub-systems.

This case is particularly interesting, since producing a coating on such a product (an intermediate between a raw material and a finished item) with the aid of a machine is a new requirement, and demands a clear view of the relevant technology. The technical process with all its possible alternatives and problems is the centre of interest. The importance of thinking about the TP is made clearer and the description of the design procedure concentrates on the concept formulation phase.

Identification of the part through the problem is assisted by the scheme of Figure 3-1, which shows the individual steps in the context of the appropriate design phases.

Introduction

A manufacturer of processed foods wishes to mechanize (use a mechanical device under human control) or automate (use a self-regulating mechanical device) a part of a manufacturing process. The task is to coat a small, flat, cylindrical product with a powder. As examples, hamburger patties, fish cakes or similar items will be covered with a suitable mixture of breadcrumbs, pepper, fennel and other spices. For this purpose, a special machine is to be developed and manufactured as a one-off device.

A first view of the proposed manufacturing process can be stated as follows: the semi-finished product (the pre-form) is made by extrusion, at the rate of about one piece per second. The cylindrical part can fall directly from the extruder on to the coating machine, and after receiving its coating it should be delivered to a conveyor belt, and transported for wrapping and packaging. The forming process takes place below room temperature, because the mixture to be extruded has a higher strength at lower temperatures, and the surface remains somewhat tacky.

The total costs of development, manufacture and test running, up to delivery of the machine, should be limited to about SwFr 70 000.

Problem Assignment

1 Aim: elaborate or clarify the assigned specification

1.1 Critically recognize the assigned problem

After studying the problem statement, the design engineer visits the manufacturer, has the production process demonstrated, and pays particular attention to the manual procedure for coating the pre-form. Conversations with the manufacturer's personnel yield important information regarding requirements, possibilities, constraints, and other conditions affecting this task. Emphasis is given to the technology of coating, the possible degree of mechanization or automation, and economic constraints.

1.2 Establish the state of the art

Comprehensive enquiries in various countries show that no similar machines, devices or aids are available. Generally such coatings are applied by hand, and a reasonably complete cover is achieved by rolling and kneading the pre-form on a layer of powder.

1.3 Analyse the problem situation

Based on this experience at the manufacturer's works, a number of possibilities occur to the designer, particularly for replacing the manual processes by mechanical processes which are at least as good. The degree of possible mechanization or automation cannot be properly assessed in these essentially mental processes, and the solutions considered are in no way lacking in problems.

1.4 Examine the possibilities of realization

The central problem of producing this coating lies in finding a suitable method (technology) that can be mechanized. Since the designer is uncertain about the technology he plans an initial study project to explore this new area before embarking on the major design work.

Few problems are foreseen in designing and manufacturing this device, because the individual

Figure 3-1

Steps from General Model according to Figure 0.1	Step	Progress of case	Design documents
1 Aim: elaborate or clarify the assigned specification	1.1 1.2 1.3 1.4 1.5 1.6 1.7	(Problem Assignment) (3-2) (3-3)	Design Specification Costs, Timetable
2 Aim: establish the functional structures	2.1 2.2 2.3 2.4 2.5 2.6 2.7	(3-4) (3-5) (-6,7) (-9,10,11,12) (-14,15,16) (3-8) (3-13) (3-13A) (3-20) (3-17)(3-18ABCD)	Black Box Diagram Sequence of Operations Technology-Representations Technical Process
3 Aim: establish the concepts	3.1 3.2 3.3 3.4 3.5	Partial System: Press Chamber (3-21) (3-19)	Concepts Optimum Concept
4 Aim: establish the preliminary layouts	4.1 4.2 4.3 4.4 4.5 4.6	Partial Systems (3-22) (3-23)	Rough Form Determination Preliminary Layout
5 Aim: establish the dimensional layouts	5.1 5.2 5.3 5.4 5.5 5.6		
6 Aim: detailing, elaboration	6.1 6.2 6.3 6.4 6.5 6.6 6.7	(3-24)(3-25)	Completed Covering Machine

3-2

Design Specification		PROJECT: Powder-Coating Machine	Fixed Req.	Desire
WDK	Sheet 1/1			
Purpose : Coating Pre-forms with various materials			×	
Operand: Pre-forms Material: Meat, Fish, Meat paste/stuffing Dimensions: φ 80 × 40 mm Weight: X g. Consistency: soft				
Operand: Covering Material: pepper, fennel, chives, etc Size: granular				
Process: Capacity: 1 preform per second Coating: uniform, thin, complete Small deformation of pre-form			× × ×	
Operation: Low number of stoppages from jamming Simple and easy cleaning Life at least 5 years (daily use) Energy: electric Transportability: on wheels			× ×	
Use: Servicing only when operation irregular Safety against operator damage/injury			× ×	
Appearance: Suited to the operating space Surfaces: polished stainless steel			× ×	
Manufacture: 1 off (or small batch)			×	×
Price: < P SFr				
Patents: no patent protection desired				
Standards & Law: materials for food processing incl. lubricants etc.			×	
Exclude contaminants			×	

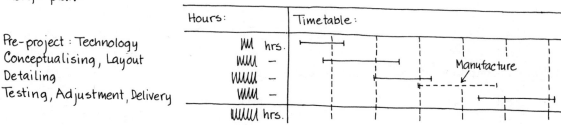

3-3 Cost breakdown :

Establishing Technology , Experiments   MMM SFr.
Design , Representation   MMMMM —
Manufacture and Assembly   MMMMMM —
Testing , Adjusting , Delivery   MMMMM —
                                           ─────────────
                                           60.000 SFr.

Rough plan :

	Hours :	Timetable :
Pre-project : Technology	MM hrs.	
Conceptualising , Layout	MMM —	Manufacture
Detailing	MMMMM —	
Testing , Adjustment , Delivery	MMM —	
	MMMMM hrs.	

functions required are within the realms of the state of the art, even though they have not been synthesized into a single machine before. Given this favourable assessment, financing for manufacture of the device is readily available to the sponsor.

1.5 Complete the requirements, classify and quantify, set priorities

1.6 Work out the full design specification (list of requirements)

Comments refer to combined use of steps 1.5 and 1.6.

The designer generates a list of requirements, as shown in Figure 3-2. In this case, as knowledge of the technology is lacking, the Design Specification is not as accurate and complete as in Cases 1 and 2. Working out even such a sketchy specification aids the designer in many ways, particularly when establishing and clarifying the ideas brought to the project by the contractors.

During the later work, other additional requirements will be discovered, and these must be discussed by the designer and the food manufacturer as they arise. (In this example, these additional requirements will not be entered into the list.)

1.7 Prepare and plan for problem solving

An outline plan and timetable are shown in Figure 3-3. As has been stated above, an initial study will clarify the technology. Further progress on this problem will depend at least in part on the results of this investigation.

Design specification

2 Aim: establish the functional structures

2.1 Abstract: produce the black box representations

A 'black box' representation of the process is shown in Figure 3-4. The inputs (mixture, and coating material) are to be transformed into the output (covered pre-forms).

2.2 Establish the technological principles Establish the sequence of operations

The surface of the pre-form to be coated is moist or fatty, which suggests that the coating material will stick to it. Adhesion can only be achieved with certainty if the coating is pressed on to the surface. The process of coating therefore consists of two activities: (a) distributing the coating material over the surface, and (b) pressing.

These two operations can be performed either in that sequence or simultaneously, as indicated in Figure 3-5. Figures 3-6 and 3-7 show how the designer represents his ideas of the technological principles; many of these proposals combine both distribution and adhesion of the covering.

The proposals must now be tested by experiment. Trials on the semi-finished product show clearly that because of their strength and stickiness the pre-forms may be manipulated, but only with great care. The designer consequently pays attention to those methods that avoid manipulation. The results of the

3-4 Black box process Model:

Pre-form / Coating material → Pre-form receives coating → Coated Pre-form (Product)

3-5

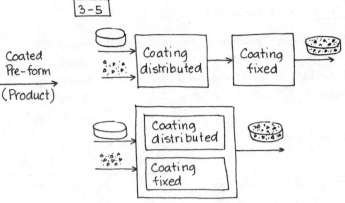

3-6 Technological Principles: Coating distribution

A: Local addition: Rolling: Spraying: Rolling on: Turning:

B: Total addition: Electrostatic: Heaped coating material: Air eddy:

3-7 Technological Principles: Coating Fixing

A: Surface Forces   Weight   Pressing: Multisided pressing:

B: Field Forces   Projectile: Electrostatic field: Centrifugal Forces

3-8 Technical Process:

Container / Pre-form / Coating → Pre-form surrounded by coating material → Container contents under pressure → Container contents separated → Container / Coated pre-form / Surplus coating material

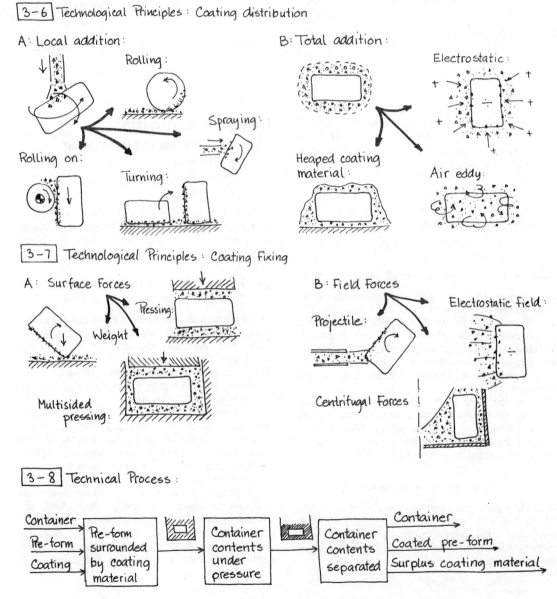

tests are evaluated against criteria such as: adhesion, distribution, appearance, and deformation of the pre-form. The tests show that some of the methods tested deliver usable products, and 'multi-sided pressing' leads to consistently good quality. The designer selects this as a basis further work on developing the TP.

2.3 Establish the technical processes,
TP → optimal TP

Technical Processes are now considered and depicted at various levels of abstraction. In this example, three TPs are generated. The first of these is a relatively abstract TP based on the technology of Figure 3-7,

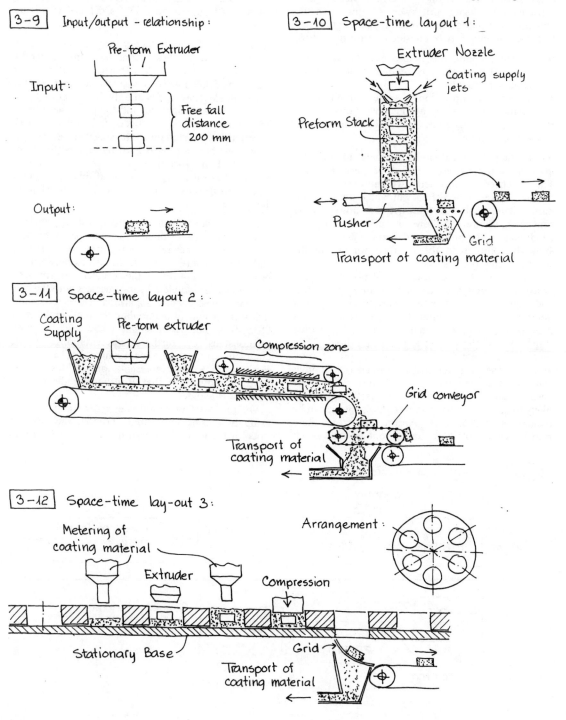

3-9 Input/output - relationship:

Pre-form Extruder

Input:

Free fall distance 200 mm

Output:

3-10 Space-time layout 1:

Extruder Nozzle

Coating supply jets

Preform Stack

Pusher   Grid

Transport of coating material

3-11 Space-time layout 2:

Coating Supply   Pre-form extruder   Compression zone

Grid conveyor

Transport of coating material

3-12 Space-time lay-out 3:

Metering of coating material   Arrangement:

Extruder   Compression

Stationary Base   Grid

Transport of coating material

where the tool for the process 'multi-sided pressing' is to be a container (more abstractly, an enclosed space) in which the mixture surrounded by coating material is to be 'compressed'. A representation of this process appears in Figure 3-8.

The solutions so far are likely to be too abstract and ambiguous, so it is useful to insert another stage to consider technological principles. At this stage the dimensions of space and time appear significant. Possible solutions may be considered with respect to:

● movement: continuous vs discontinuous motion
● number of work stations: multi-station vs single-station construction
● progress of operations: some simultaneous operations vs no simultaneous operations
● geometric arrangement: linear vs circular arrangement of stations

At this stage the verbal model is difficult to evaluate, involving as it does the dimensions of space and time. There is a need for more detailed comprehension. The designer makes some sketches in which the machine parts figure only as abstractions and outline principles. Figure 3-9 shows the input and output conditions of the process, and Figures 3-10 to 3-12 show the solutions in abstract form for the 'multi-sided pressing' process.

Evaluations of these ideas are not possible in the abstract. The designer must once again plan, lay out, and request the manufacture of various experimental items to perform appropriate tests. These experiments must be kept simple, so that the financial and time framework of the project is not jeopardized. They serve to establish orders of magnitude of press forces, and show that it is not possible to generate enough force by feed motions (as in Figure 3-11). The designer thus selects solution 3-12 as the one most likely to be satisfactory, and recognizes that it can be realized in many ways. Abstracting from these principles, the designer then produces the block

diagram of the optimum technical process, Figure 3-13.

A third cycle of detail in considering the TP follows from Figure 3-13. The designer uses the technological principles of Figure 3-14 (items A, B, C and D), to produce Figure 3-13A. This cycle starts with determining and selecting the technological principles and operations from Figure 3-13, as detailed in Figure 3-14.

[A question of design theory may be raised here, namely whether these considerations generally establish function-carriers (partial solutions for organs) as defined in *Principles*. The authors' answer is that the sketches represent only the technology, the action of tool or machine, and the processed object. From these sketches the effects or functions can be seen; and this is an aid for a later stage, to suggest how these functions can be realized by organs (function-carriers). It is fortuitous if these considerations provide detailed design solutions at this stage, but it may be dangerous to by-pass the following steps in this phase.]

A decision about the various technological principles involved is not immediately possible, partly because of the unknown behaviour of the processed materials and partly because of the relationships between the principles. For this reason the designer performs tests to examine the individual sub-processes with the help of simple experimental apparatus. These tests show that it is possible to manipulate the pre-forms with a lifting fork. The design engineer now tests the inter-relationships by further representations of the complete arrangement; see Figures 3-15 and 3-16. Both space vs time representations of this process have the advantage that transporting the coating material is avoided.

On the basis of additional experiments and an evaluation using appropriate criteria, the designer opts for the technology shown in Figure 3-16. From

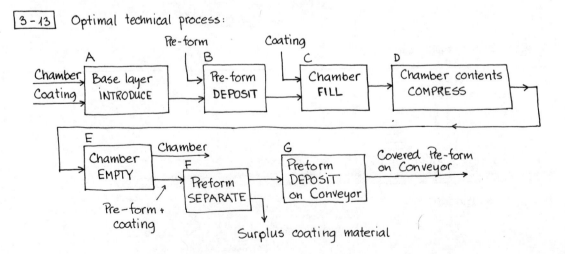

3-13 Optimal technical process:

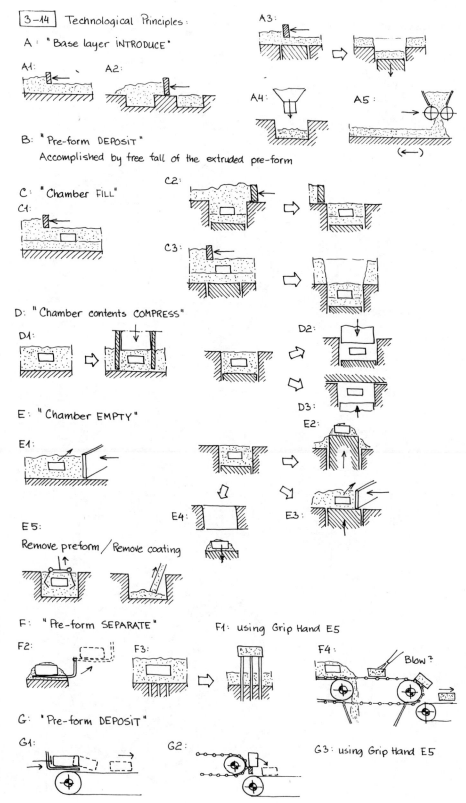

3–14 Technological Principles:

A: "Base layer INTRODUCE"

A1:   A2:   A3:

A4:   A5:

(←)

B: "Pre-form DEPOSiT"
Accomplished by free fall of the extruded pre-form

C: "Chamber FILL"
C1:   C2:

C3:

D: "Chamber contents COMPRESS"

D1:   D2:

D3:

E: "Chamber EMPTY"

E1:   E2:

E4:   E3:

E5:

Remove preform / Remove coating

F: "Pre-form SEPARATE"   F1: using Grip Hand E5

F2:   F3:   F4:   Blow?

G: "Pre-form DEPOSiT"

G1:   G2:   G3: using Grip Hand E5

3-15 Space-Time Layout of Process 1 :

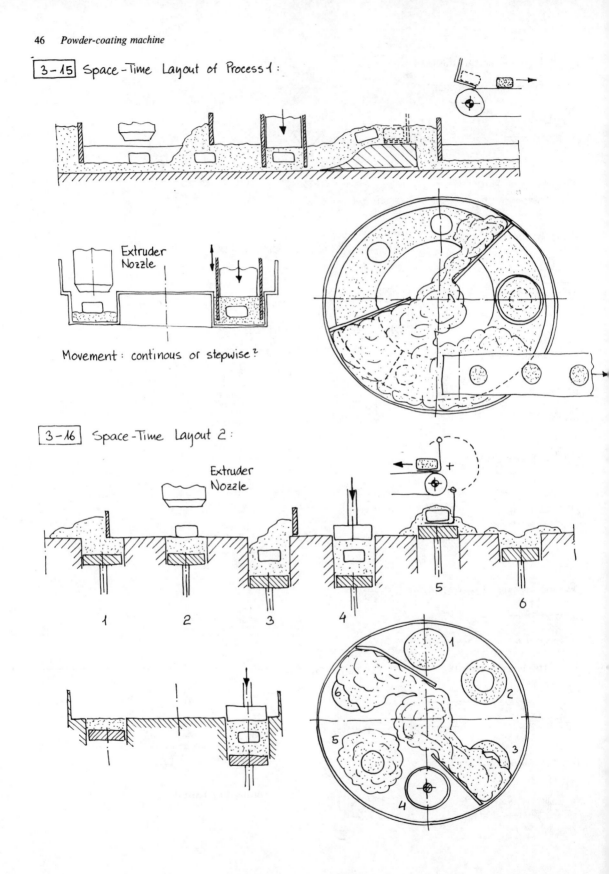

Extruder
Nozzle

Movement: continous or stepwise?

3-16 Space-Time Layout 2 :

Extruder
Nozzle

1   2   3   4   5   6

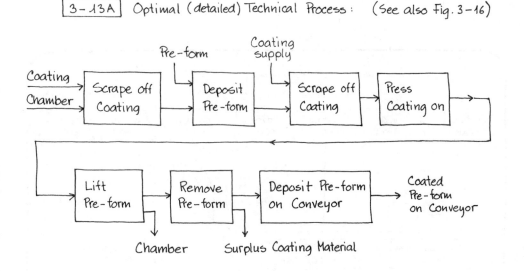

3-13A Optimal (detailed) Technical Process: (See also Fig. 3-16)

this picture he can now derive the detailed TP, and represent it as in Figure 3-13A. This figure should be a good basis for establishing the functional structure.

2.4 Apply technical systems to the process, and establish boundaries

2.5 Establish the grouping of functions

Comments refer to combined use of steps 2.4 and 2.5.

A major requirement is that all operations should be mechanized, and that the machine should work automatically. The boundaries of the machine system are therefore defined: (a) at the input – delivery of the pre-form from the extruder to the machine; (b) at the output – transfer of the coated product to the conveyor belt.

It is arguable that it might be useful or even preferable to perform operations A–E and F–G (Figures 3-13 and 3-14) by two separate machines, but a single machine could be made to perform all operations from the input to the output. The designer decides at this stage that the whole process will be performed by one machine.

2.6 Establish the functional structures, and represent them

Starting from Figure 3-13A, the designer develops the functional structure, Figure 3-17, which describes in fairly concrete terms the current selection of technologies. As compared to other examples in this book, abstract formulations of functional structure are not

necessary because the relevant concrete solution proposals have already been decided. Various groupings of functions are possible, particularly with respect to the propulsion. Four variants are represented in Figure 3-18, as alternatives to the relevant parts of Figure 3-17.

2.7 Σ Functional structures
   Improve Evaluate, decide Verify

Based on the desire to produce a robust mechanical system, the designer selects Variant B of Figure 3-18 as the optimal functional structure, namely using the table rotation to drive both the chamber ram and the fork system.

Optimal functional structure

3 Aim: establish the concepts

In this case study, the authors do not wish to show the work involved in the steps of searching for function-carriers and basic arrangements. Figure 3-19 shows the concept selected by the designer for this machine. From this diagram one can see that both the circular table and the fork system are driven from a single motor and that the motion of the chamber ram is derived from the table rotation (compare functional structure B, Figure 3-18). The pressing force is produced by a pneumatic cylinder. The fork system is relatively complicated, using a repeated transfer movement, and employing a geared transmission.

3-17 Functional Structure:

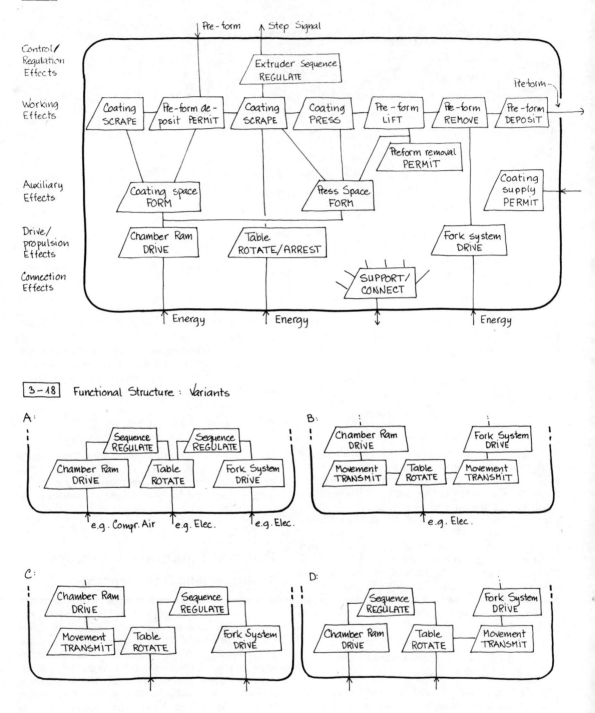

3-18 Functional Structure: Variants

3-19 Concept (partial)

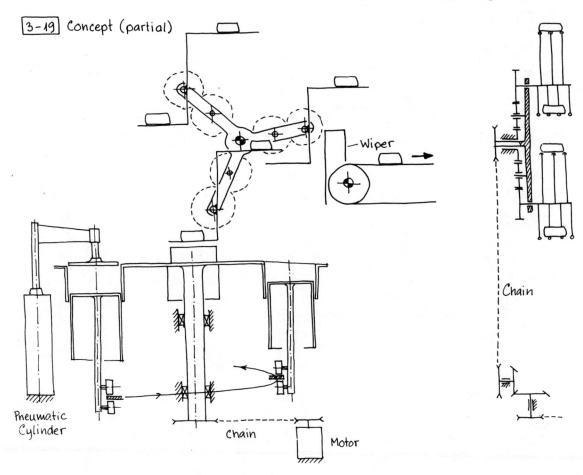

Wiper

Chain

Pneumatic
Cylinder

Chain

Motor

3-20 List of functions for Press Chamber System:

Chamber of variable
depth FORM ....
{
Ram GUIDE

Drive PERMIT

Coating and Pre-form
STORE ....
{
Chamber Wall FORM

Ram FORM

Chamber SEAL

Cleaning PERMIT ⟶ Ram Disassembly PERMIT

Pre-form MOVE into
contact with
Fork System ....
{
Engaging of
Pre-form PERMIT

3-21 Concepts of Press Chamber System :

"Ram GUIDE" :

"Ram SEAL" :

Tolerance :

"Drive PERMIT" / "Disassembly PERMIT" :

Engaging of Pre-form PERMIT" :

Concepts :

A :   B :   C :

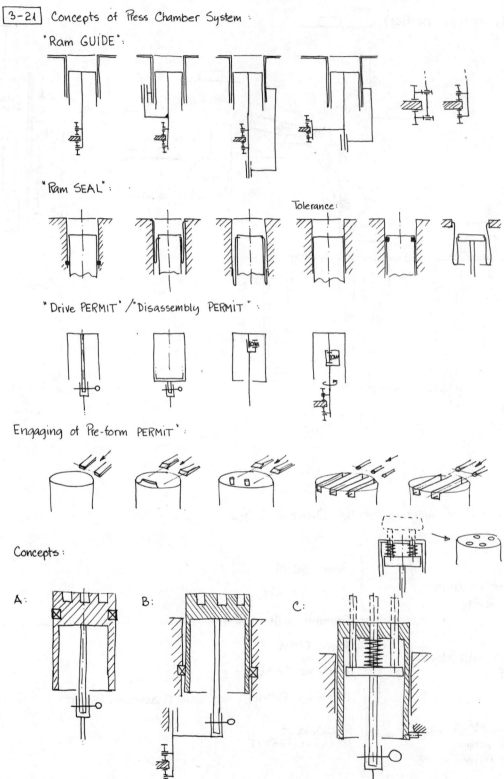

Design of a sub-system – press chamber

The following sections do not follow the layout of the whole system. The machine is complex, so the designer must concentrate on one partial system after another, finally producing a total layout. The press chamber system is selected as an example, and shown by a simplified description. The first steps of formulating a design specification are omitted, as indicated by the dashed upward-curved line in Figure 3-1.

The press chamber consists of two major parts, the cylindrical chamber mounted on the circular table and the ram driven by a cam rail. Its functions are:

- to form a chamber of variable depth
- to store coating material and a pre-form of the product
- to provide the reaction to the forces from the compression plate
- to move the product to contact the fork system

The means of performing these functions are shown in the concept in Figure 3-19. This sub-system must now be completed, basing the discussions of alternatives and preferable solutions on the list of requirements and the secondary functions necessary for the press chamber.

2   Aim: establish the functional structure (press chamber)

Since the press chamber sub-system is now established

in an identifiable form, the designer can proceed to establish the functional structure (see Figure 3-20). The designer decides that it is essential to be able to remove the ram to allow cleaning and the usual hygiene procedures.

3   Aim: establish the concept (press chamber)

Instead of using a morphological matrix, the designer decides to generate the concept of the press chamber by considering, in sketch form, the critical zones and their combinations, as in Figure 3-21.

[This approach is permissible because the general procedural model cannot be a rigid set of rules; it must give the designer the necessary flexibility, but at the same time help to ensure complete, thorough and yet creative work. This departure from the general model presented in *Principles* is useful here, because the problems are of a relatively minor nature and quick conceptualizing of solutions is needed.]

4   Establish the preliminary layout (press chamber)

4.1   Establish the orientation points for form determination

The designer selects concept **B** in Figure 3-21 as preferable. Important points in the form design of the proposed components are the diameter of the cylinder, the stroke, the distance between the

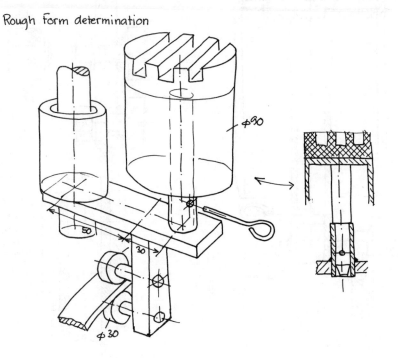

| 3-22 | Rough form determination

guideway and the cylinder axis, and the size of the rollers. Again, the designer establishes the dimensions with the aid of simple experiments.

4.2   Establish the arrangements, investigate re-use, rough form-giving, partial dimensioning

The designer feels that further structural variations are not useful and continues with the selected structure: variant B, Figure 3-21. Standard solutions for the sealing ring, a linear ball bearing for guidance, and a standard roller element are used. This outline form-determination with only partial dimensioning is shown in Figure 3-22.

4.3   Establish the types of material, classes of manufacturing method, tolerances and surface properties where necessary

Based on the requirements for materials used in machinery for the food industry, the designer selects nylon for the ram head, and stainless steel for the ram and cylinder. The other parts will be manufactured

from steel, and electroplated. The designer sees no reason to concern himself with tolerances at this stage.

4.4   Investigate the critical form-determination zones

The designer finds no particular problems with the actions of this sub-system, but he anticipates that cleaning with acid or alkaline solutions, even though weak, might create problems.

4.5   Represent the preliminary layout

The preliminary layout is sketched in Figure 3-23, with alternatives for some partial solutions.

Other sub-systems

Other sub-systems are treated in a similar manner to that used for the press chamber. The details are left to the reader.

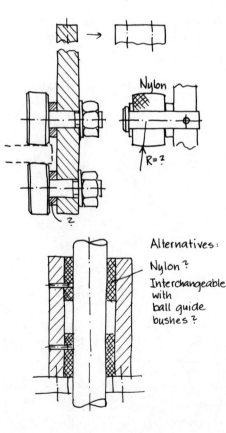

| 3-23 | Preliminary Layout :

3-24

3-25

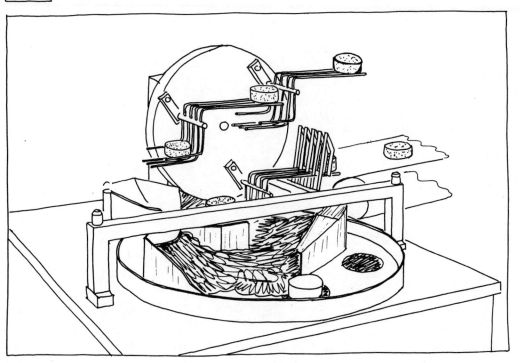

The results of this case study are shown in views of the completed coating machine. Figure 3-24 shows the total machine system under test. The chambers, circular table and fork system are visible, but the conveyor band system for transporting the coated pre-form is not shown. Figure 3-25 shows the circular table, with the coating material, the pre-form in its starting position, and the coated product on the transfer forks.

Concluding steps 4.5 to 6.7 are not developed for this case.

Case 4   P–V–T apparatus

Experimental and demonstration apparatus for visible boiling and condensation in the vicinity of the critical point

This case study shows the application of the systematic design method to a technical system, where some approximate 'worst case' calculations are necessary during evaluation. The design process is divided into small steps, but the sequence and emphasis are modified because of the particular circumstances of the design problem. For instance, the designer finds it preferable to make sequential decisions on the basis of the calculations and other criteria, because these decisions can be fairly objective. In the phases of design completion following those presented here, rating schemes similar to those used in other case studies in this book are employed by the designer to aid decision making on more subjective issues.

Figure 4-1 gives an overview of the procedure, and refers to the design documents up to the preliminary layout. Each step is accompanied by comments, descriptive statements of the design considerations and results, and calculations where appropriate.

Introduction

A thermodynamics professor in the engineering faculty of a university is planning to have a simple apparatus made in-house. It is intended to be operated by students, and should permit them to (1) see and watch the processes of boiling and condensation in a homogeneous fluid, especially around the critical point, and (2) measure the variables needed to generate a pressure–volume–temperature diagram (P–V–T curves). A sequence of laboratory exercises would result in one curve per group of students in the class, and the class would thus generate a set of curves to cover the ranges of the variables. This experiment should provide a means by which the professor can interest and motivate the students, but this aspect is generally outside the scope of the designer's work on this project. It is the duty of the teaching staff to formulate the laboratory instructions for such an experiment, and to provide the guidance and enthusiasm in their interactions with the students. However, the methods of operating this device and the way it performs its tasks should not detract from these considerations.

Problem assignment

1   Aim: elaborate or clarify the assigned specification

1.1   Critically recognize the assigned problem

The designer recognizes that a sufficiently large quantity of a suitable fluid must be contained in a transparent vessel to allow direct observation of the fluid. The most important considerations are safety and simplicity of operation, including clearly visible relationships between the measuring facilities and the variables. Measuring accuracy is of secondary importance.

1.2   Establish the state of the art

Experimental apparatus of greater accuracy is available, but it is totally enclosed and does not permit direct observation of the working fluid.

1.3   Analyse the problem situation

The basis for evaluation of possible solutions is the skill and ability of an average second-year student, and the following educational objectives: (1) the student should understand the processes (mechanical, hydraulic, thermodynamic and others), and (2) the student should gain experience in manipulating simple measuring equipment. The following points are therefore considered:

(a) Quick reading of the measurement is more important than accuracy, particularly if 'trade-offs' between these factors lead to added complexity.
(b) Maintenance and preparation of the apparatus is to be done by trained technical assistants.
(c) Long-term stability of readings must be ensured within the limits of accuracy of the measuring apparatus, at least for about 3 months.

Figure 4-1

Steps from General Model according to Figure 0.1	Step	Progress of case	Design documents
1 Aim: elaborate or clarify the assigned specification	1.1 1.2 1.3 1.4 1.5 1.6 1.7		Main Requirements State of Art Criteria, Constraints Realization Possibilities Design Specification
2 Aim: establish the functional structures	2.1 2.2 2.3 2.4 2.5 2.6 2.7		TP Black Box Diagram TP Principle TD Block Diagram Groupings Functional Structure
3 Aim: establish the concepts	3.1 3.2 3.3 3.4 3.5		Inputs, Outputs Morphological Matrix Function-Carriers Relationships Optimal Concept
4 Aim: establish the preliminary layouts	4.1 4.2 4.3 4.4 4.5 4.6		Arrangement, Rough Form Some Sizes.
5 Aim: establish the dimensional layouts	5.1 5.2 5.3 5.4 5.5 5.6		
6 Aim: detailing, elaboration	6.1 6.2 6.3 6.4 6.5 6.6 6.7		

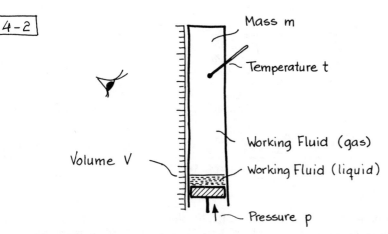

4-2

Mass m

Temperature t

Working Fluid (gas)

Working Fluid (liquid)

Volume V

Pressure p

(d) There must be a minimum tendency for any part of the apparatus to change position unless required (self-locking should occur against the influences of stored potential energy, e.g. by friction), and a minimum chance of uncontrolled actions which might affect any inputs or adjustments that a student may make.

Only bought-out parts will be charged to capital budgets for the fixed costs of manufacturing the apparatus. Manufacture in the university workshops from materials and parts existing in the workshops is regarded as free. Running costs for the completed apparatus (fluids, spare parts, etc.) will be charged to operating budgets.

Finding a suitable fluid is a crucial problem. The choice of fluid will allow the designer to establish the ranges of properties, measurement variables, and minimum dimensions of the observation chamber for the proposed apparatus. Constraints include:

(a) The working fluid should have low toxicity and flammability, in case of failure.
(b) High pressures and temperatures should be avoided, shielded or contained.

[This search for a working fluid requires a change from the procedural model. The apparatus will not be feasible if a suitable fluid cannot be found. Fixing a solution at this stage is generally too early in the design process for effective and creative work.]

4-3

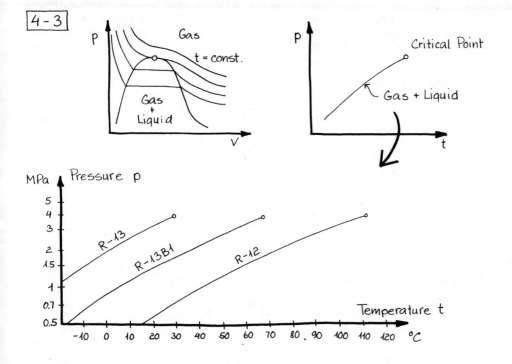

Table 4-1   Comparison of fluids

Fluid		Critical temperature t_c (°C)	Critical pressure p_c (°C) (kPa)	Bottle size	Price
R-13B1	$CBrF_3$	67.0	3964	4.5 kg	Can$ 331.78
R-13	$CClF_3$	28.85	3870	4.1 kg	Can$ 467.82
R-41	CH_3F	44.60	5877		
Nitrous oxide	N_2O	36.5	7265		
(R-1)	CCl_2F_2	111.5	4012	14 kg	Can$ 80.72

Comparative prices quoted by DuPont Canada Ltd (trade mark 'Freon') in September 1982. Similar halogen carbon compounds are also available from other manufacturers.

1.4   Examine the possibilities of realization

The designer must find a working fluid which has its critical temperature within a readily accessible working range, say 20 to 90°C (preferably around 60°C), and critical pressure between 100 kPa (about 1 atmosphere) and 10 MPa.

Reference 4.1, p. 31-32, shows that at least 14 such fluids exist. The most suitable of these are listed in Table 4-1, together with some comparative prices (quoted by DuPont Canada Ltd, September 1982). The main features of the P–V–T relationships are shown in Figure 4-3.

Further data may be found in the manufacturer's publications (e.g. see reference 4.2). Similar halogen-carbon compounds are also available from other manufacturers. Sample data for the two-phase saturated state of the most suitable two of these fluids are shown in Table 4-2.

Comparing these two fluids shows that the compound R-13 would have to be cooled below room temperature to reach an adequate sub-critical range.

Fluid R-13B1 shows a higher volume ratio, and lower latent heat, at somewhat higher pressures than R-13, and can provide usable experimental results between room temperature and about 90°C. Consequently the designer chooses the fluid R-13B1.

[Note that the designer uses a sound approach to problem-solving. Each of these considerations is separated into smaller steps: the problem is well defined; many possibilities are generated or found; evaluation and selection take place.]

Typical approximate values for the superheated state are available from reference 4.2 and are summarized in Table 4-3.

The largest available volume ratio in the assumed experimental range is about 310:1, and may be found from values of specific volume at the limiting conditions: liquid, 20°C; gaseous, 90°C, 100 kPa. A minimum height of fluid should be chosen to ensure that the liquid phase is visible: 5 mm minimum, preferably 10 mm.

Table 4-2   Saturation properties of two fluids

Temperature, t (°C)	Pressure, p (kPa)	Density		Enthalpy, latent, h (kJ/kg)	Volume ratio, gas/liquid
		Liquid (kg/m³)	Gas (kg/m³)		
R-13: critical volume 205 cm³/mol, molecular weight 104.5					
28.85	3870		577.8	0	1
20	3170.8	921.5	264.2	56.67	3.49
10	2517.6	1036.1	184.7	75.02	5.62
0	1945.5	1118.7	135.1	88.31	8.28
R-13B1: critical volume 180 cm³/mol, molecular weight 148.9					
67.0	3963.8		744.9	0	1
60	3459.8	1146.4	378.2	40.38	3.03
50	2825.5	1303.4	268.2	56.15	4.86
40	2280.9	1411.7	200.0	67.22	7.06
30	1821.6	1499.0	151.7	75.97	9.88
20	1433.4	1574.5	115.6	83.32	13.62

Table 4-3 Superheated properties of fluid R-13B1

Pressure, p (kPa)		Temperature, t (°C)								t_s (°C)
		20	30	40	50	60	70	80	90	
4000	ϱ	–	–	–	–	–	433	355	314	Super-
	h	–	–	–	–	–	129	139	147	critical
3000	ϱ	–	–	–	–	260	229	212	199	
	h	–	–	–	–	136	145	150	156	53
2000	ϱ	–	–	163	149	138	129	123	118	
	h	–	–	133	140	147	153	158	163	34
1000	ϱ	72	69	66	63	60	57	55	54	
	h	134	137	143	148	154	160	166	169	6
500	ϱ	37	31	30	29	28	27	26	25	
	h	138	142	146	152	157	163	167	171	–18
100	ϱ	6.3	6.1	5.9	5.7	5.5	5.3	5.2	5.1	
	h	141	146	149	154	159	165	171	173	–58

ϱ Density (kg/m^3)
h Specific heat (enthalpy) (kJ/kg)
t_s Saturation temperature (°C) at pressure p

1.5 Complete the requirements, classify and quantify, set priorities

1.6 Work out the full design specification (list of requirements)

Comments refer to combined use of steps 1.5 and 1.6.

The result of the designer's considerations up to this stage is shown in the design specification, Table 4-4.

1.7 Prepare and plan for problem-solving

The designer finds that the critical areas of this problem seem to be in establishing the modes of action and the form of certain parts of the technical system. At this stage it is too early to recognize which parts will need particular attention. It is decided that the procedural plan will be developed and adapted as the design work proceeds, keeping as close as possible to the procedural model of Figure 0-1.

Design specification

2 Aim: establish the functional structures

2.1 Abstract: produce the black box representations

A 'black box' diagram of the process is shown in Figure 4-4. The designer, on reviewing the design specification, forms the opinion that the requirements of visual observation and measurement are so important that he includes them in a revised black box diagram, Figure 4-4A.

2.2 Establish the technological principles
Establish the sequence of operations

Each of the sub-processes shown in the revised black box diagram leads to a choice of technologies. One in particular, the technology of 'Generating a new state', needs to be investigated in more detail. The technologies described in Figure 4-5 are readily available, and observe the well-known principle of experimentation: 'change one variable at a time'.

[The representation chosen by the designer in these diagrams is not sufficiently abstract for this stage of the design process. Variant A1 should have been drawn as two boxes of different size, labelled 'p_1, V_1, t_1' and 'p_2, V_2, t_2'. This revised representation would avoid the implication that only an axial piston arrangement is available to change the volume. The next step has, in fact, compensated for this deficiency.]

Evaluation:

- Variants B1 and B2 require separate measurement of the variable 'mass', which is a disadvantage of these solutions.
- Variant A2 needs changes of temperature within short time intervals; these depend largely on the heat contents of the components.
- The designer considers variant A1 to be optimal.

2.3 Establish the technical processes,
TP → optimal TP

The thoughts about the process to be realized and the operations to be performed are collected in the process structure, Figure 4-6. It is clear from the properties of the working fluid, compound R-13B1, that the apparatus being designed will need to be

Table 4-4 List of requirements (design specification)

	Fixed req.	Desire
1 *Main functional purpose*		
Condensation and boiling (Technical Process) of the homogeneous fluid R-13B1 (Operand) near the critical point, such that the processes can be observed directly by eye, and suitable quantities (pressure, volume, and temperature, etc.) can be measured, as a laboratory exercise for students.	*	
Use within a laboratory environment, usual room temperature about 20°C, air conditioned, relative humidity about 70%, etc.	*	
2 *Functionally determined properties*		
Use and operation by persons with skill levels as expected for students.	*	
Apparatus as clear and uncluttered as possible.		*
Simple adjustment, setting and reading.		*
Direct measurement (if possible no intermediate stages), some limitations on accuracy permitted.		*
2A *Additional condition (added at step 2.3)*		
Chamber volume must be reducible to zero, with no dead spaces, to ensure minimum contamination of the working fluid as it is filled into the chamber.	*	
2B *Additional conditions (added at step. 3.3b)*		
Interior of apparatus must have provisions for vacuum out-gassing of surfaces before filling with transfer fluid (mercury).	*	
Transfer fluid (mercury) must be vacuum de-gassed immediately before being introduced into apparatus.	*	
3 *Operational properties*		
At least ten P–V–T settings and measurements attainable per hour, assuming 2 to 3 hours in the laboratory for each group.	*	
Preferably no external energy sources for main motions.		*
Compressed air at 400 kPa, domestic electric supply at 110 V, 60 Hz, 15 A, and hot and cold running water are available.		
3.1 *Reliability*		
Long-term stability is needed, at least over the teaching term (or semester) within the selected measuring accuracy.	*	
3.2 *Service life*		
At least ten years, with annual maintenance and preparation for use.		*
3.3 *Maintainability*		
Maintenance and preparation as simple as possible, but will be performed by trained personnel.		*
3.4 *Space requirements*		
Small space, table-top mountable, easy storage in under-bench cupboard when not in use.	*	
4 *Ergonomic properties*		
Placement of TS input organs and indicators to be within preferred ergonomic space for operators.	*	
Capabilities of a 15- to 18-year-old with respect to force and power should be adequate.	*	
Sufficiently pleasant operating environment.		*
4.1 *Optimum MS capability*		
Clear, easily readable indicators, preferably at eye level, and visible from the operating location.	*	

Table 4-4 *(Continued)*

4.2 *Safety*
Non-toxic and non-flammable materials, pressures and temperatures perferably *
within easily attainable ranges, shielding to contain breakages, no hazardous
surfaces exposed to personal contact, self-locking of adjustment and setting
motions.

5 *Appearance*
Simple external form encouraging easy use, otherwise appearance is not *
particularly important.

6 *Distribution properties*
Transportation to the laboratory (0.5 km outdoors) will be needed. *

7 *Delivery and organizational planning*
Ready for 1983/84 academic year, including operating instructions and a sample *
test run by staff.

8 *Law and standards*
Safety and inspection requirements laid down by statute. *

9 *Manufacture*
Own workshops, machine tools, welding, sheet metal machinery, etc. (except *
special parts).

10 *Economics*
'First costs', materials and labour are free of charge. Special parts and pre- *
finished components must be obtained through the departmental capital
budget. Costs must not exceed $2000 (Canadian).
Running costs, materials etc. must be obtained through the departmental *
operating budget. Less than $100 (Canadian) per year.

General design properties *
Corrosion, effects on environment, etc.
Preferably no damaging changes, easy cleaning.
No leakage of harmful fluids. *

4-4

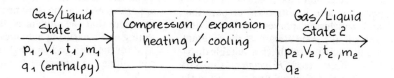

4-4A

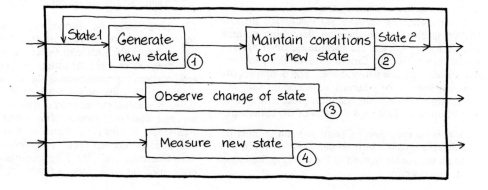

4 – 5

TECHNOLOGY ① : $q_1 \rightarrow q_2$ by equalizing (heat transfer) after settings.

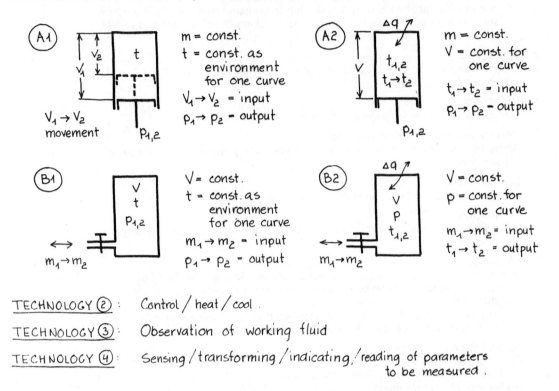

Ⓐ1

$V_1 \rightarrow V_2$
movement

$P_{1,2}$

m = const.
t = const. as
  environment
  for one curve
$V_1 \rightarrow V_2$ = input
$P_1 \rightarrow P_2$ = output

Ⓐ2

$\Delta q \nearrow$

$P_{1,2}$

m = const.
V = const. for
  one curve
$t_1 \rightarrow t_2$ = input
$P_1 \rightarrow P_2$ = output

Ⓑ1

$m_1 \rightarrow m_2$

V = const.
t = const. as
  environment
  for one curve
$m_1 \rightarrow m_2$ = input
$P_1 \rightarrow P_2$ = output

Ⓑ2

$\Delta q \nearrow$

$m_1 \rightarrow m_2$

V = const.
p = const. for
  one curve
$m_1 \rightarrow m_2$ = input
$t_1 \rightarrow t_2$ = output

TECHNOLOGY ② : Control / heat / cool.

TECHNOLOGY ③ : Observation of working fluid

TECHNOLOGY ④ : Sensing / transforming / indicating / reading of parameters
                                        to be measured.

prepared for use by introducing the fluid into the chamber under pressure, and that after use the apparatus must be stored safely. The set of experiments (the 'execution phase' of the process of using the apparatus) also has its own 'preparation', 'execution' and 'conclusion' phases. These activities are clearly visible in the main stream of the diagram. Decisions are still needed to establish a suitable distribution of the effects (see *Principles*, Glossary definition 19) of 'heating/cooling' and 'actuating the volume boundary movement' between the human operator and the machine system.

At this point, the designer has recognized the restriction implied in the diagram describing volume change, Figure 4-5, and has encouraged other options by the more abstract formulation of the problem, namely 'change chamber volume'. The design specification needs to be changed to accommodate the 'preparation' phase in the technical process structure. The addition to Table 4-4 consists of the statement:

2. **Additional conditions** Chamber volume must be reducible to zero, with no dead spaces, to ensure minimum contamination of the working fluid as it fills the chamber.

2.4 Apply technical systems to the process and establish boundaries

Complete automation of the experiment (i.e. of the apparatus and the measurements) should be avoided, to ensure that the student is directly involved in the setting and measuring activities. Automation may be used for 'heating and cooling', and for regulating and controlling the temperature within suitable limits.

2.5 Establish the grouping of functions

Groupings may be formed by considering the following parts of the total process shown in Figure 4-6 as separable functions: (a) actuating the volume and pressure change; (b) setting and controlling the temperature; (c) transforming the main operand, i.e. changing the state of the working fluid. Figure 4-7 shows possible combinations of these sub-groups into separate machine systems. The symbols in the top right-hand corners of function boxes show the connections between Figures 4-6 and 4-7.

Evaluations of these groupings cannot be performed at this stage: further information is

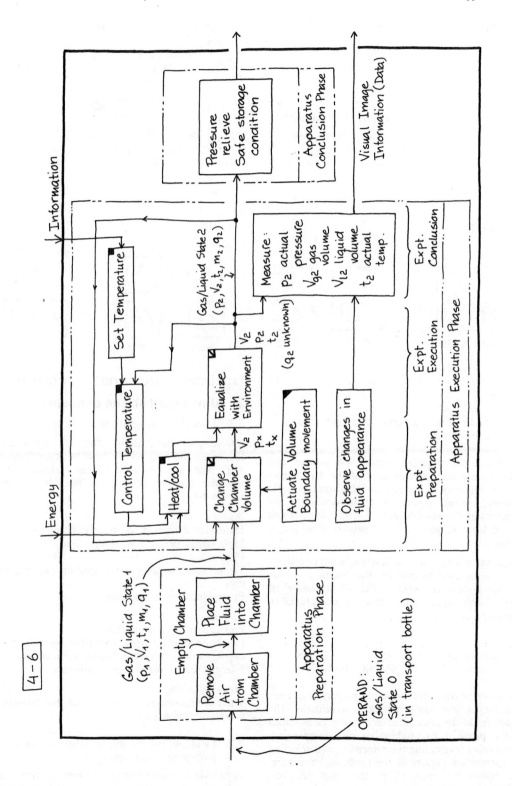

4 – 7

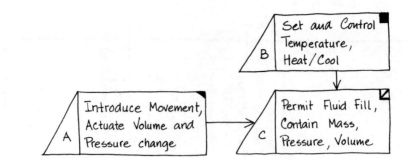

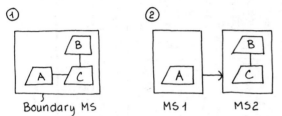

Groupings :

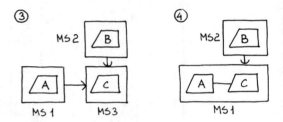

required about the functions and how they may be realized.

2.6   Establish the functional structures, and represent them

The functional structure, Figure 4-8 (drawn and labelled from the point of view of the TS), shows distinct similarity to the process structure. Possible variants have been generated by considering the implications of Figures 4-6 and 4-7, and attempting to expand their scope to permit greater freedom of action.

[It should be noted that the designer is not consistent in the verbs used to describe the functions of the machine system, i.e. whether the MS is 'active' or 'passive' with respect to the performance of a function (compare Case 1).]

2.7   Σ Functional structures
Improve   Evaluate, decide   Verify

Evaluation of the proposed solutions must wait until the concepts have been generated in some detail. The sequencing of the procedural model must be modified for this problem, by establishing the concepts in a logical order, evaluating the principles, and selecting the appropriate variant of the functional structure. The evaluations required at this step are best performed by progressing through steps 3.1 to 3.3.

Optimal functional structure

3   Aim: establish the concepts

3.1   Establish the inputs and modes of action

The designer finds it useful in this case study to restate the inputs and outputs in a brief but clear fashion to help with an overview of the problem. These statements can be added to the 'black box' diagram, Figure 4-4.

Inputs
Hand (force or moment, translation or rotation)
Light (sight, perception, observation)
Fluid mass
Temperature requirement (adjusting and maintaining)
Energy (heating or cooling)

Outputs
Pressure or force (from fluid)
Forces or moments (reactions from operation)
Display values (pressure, temperature, volume)
Energy (heat transfer to environment)

Modes of action
These are generated in the next step, and listed in the morphological matrix.

3.2   Establish the classes of function-carrier (morphological matrix)

Proposals for providing the various functions stated in Figure 4-8 are entered in the morphological matrix,

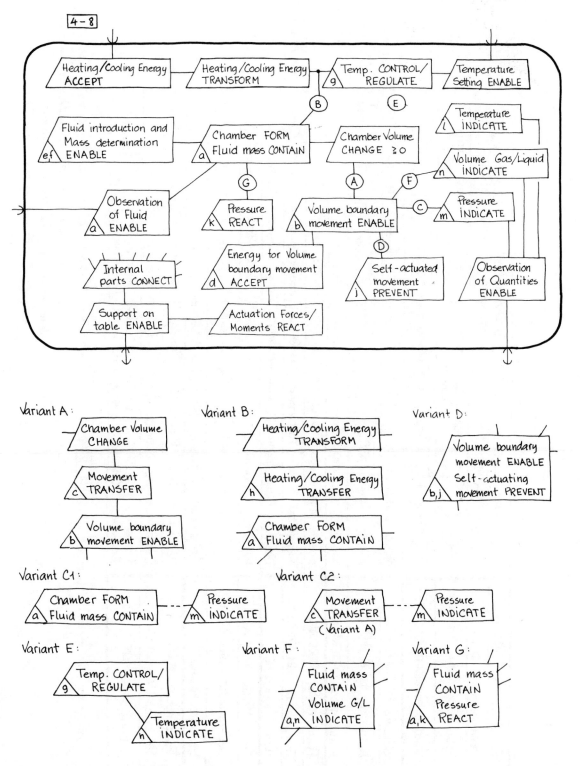

4-8

Heating/Cooling Energy ACCEPT

Heating/Cooling Energy TRANSFORM

Temp. CONTROL/ REGULATE — g

Temperature Setting ENABLE

Fluid introduction and Mass determination ENABLE — e,f

Chamber FORM Fluid mass CONTAIN — a

Chamber Volume CHANGE ≥ 0

Temperature INDICATE — l

Volume Gas/Liquid INDICATE — n

Observation of Fluid ENABLE — a

Pressure REACT — k

Volume boundary movement ENABLE — b

Pressure INDICATE — m

Internal parts CONNECT

Energy for Volume boundary movement ACCEPT — d

Self-actuated movement PREVENT — j

Observation of Quantities ENABLE

Support on table ENABLE

Actuation Forces/ Moments REACT

Variant A:
Chamber Volume CHANGE
Movement TRANSFER — c
Volume boundary movement ENABLE — b

Variant B:
Heating/Cooling Energy TRANSFORM
Heating/Cooling Energy TRANSFER — h
Chamber FORM Fluid mass CONTAIN — a

Variant D:
Volume boundary movement ENABLE Self-actuating movement PREVENT — b,j

Variant C1:
Chamber FORM Fluid mass CONTAIN — a ----- Pressure INDICATE — m

Variant C2:
Movement TRANSFER — c (Variant A) ----- Pressure INDICATE — m

Variant E:
Temp. CONTROL/ REGULATE — g
Temperature INDICATE — n

Variant F:
Fluid mass CONTAIN Volume G/L INDICATE — a,n

Variant G:
Fluid mass CONTAIN Pressure REACT — a,k

4–9

a	Fluid mass CONTAIN	One-component Transparent, Rigid	One-component Transparent, Flexible	Multi-component Transparent, Rigid	Opaque Rigid
b	Observation ENABLE	Along main axis of Chamber	Across main axis of Chamber		
	Volume boundary direction				
	Volume boundary MOVE	Piston	Plunger	Membrane	Rolling Diaphragm / Liquid Piston *
c	Movement TRANSFER	None (direct Piston → Fluid)	Solid member	Liquid intermediate member *	
d	Actuation force APPLY	Lever	Rack and Crank	Screw & Handwheel	Air or Oil Pressure
e	Fluid mass DETERMINE	Weigh	Calculate from known values (state)		
f	Fluid mass INTRODUCE	Capsule plus valves	Direct inlet through Chamber Valve		
g	Temperature SET/CONTROL	Thermostat Switch	Thermostat plus Relay	Observer plus Hand switch	Observer plus valve
h	Heat TRANSFER	Direct in Fluid	Through Chamber wall	Through Transfer Member, row "c"	
i	Heat MAKE AVAILABLE	Electric Element	Warm water (piped)	Warm water environment	
j	Self-actuated motion PREVENT	No special provisions	Friction contact	Ratchet	
k	Pressure REACT	No special provisions	Strapping	Tension bolts	
l	Temperature MEASURE	Mercury in Glass	Bimetal Strip	Bimetal Thermocouple / Thermistor	Thermodiode
m	Pressure MEASURE	Bourdon-tube Indicator	Elec. Res. Strain Gauge on Tube		
n	Volume MEASURE	Scale on Chamber	Scale in Chamber	Linear Scale on Movement Input	Rotary Scale on Movement Input / Combinations

Compare Functional Structure, Fig. 4-8

* Note to rows "b" and "c":
"Liquid Piston" and "Liquid intermediate member" were added by the design engineer as consequence of investigations in Step 3.3

Figure 4-9. The design engineer in this case has not stated the physical principles that can create an effect, but has listed the specific function-carriers required for the final product.

The functions are listed in the first column in the approximate order of importance in which they will probably need to be investigated to select the optimal combinations. This ordering constitutes a limited procedural plan for the designer. Cross-references to the functional structure are given by the letters shown in the first column, which have also been entered into Figure 4-8.

3.3 Combine the function-carriers, examine their relationships

The 'order of importance' procedural plan indicated in the morphological matrix is now followed to aid the investigations.

Problem 3.3a

The core problem at this stage is recognized as 'contain fluid mass'. The pressure of the fluid must be contained in the main body and any connecting pipes or valves, and viewing of the fluid must be possible. For visibility from all sides, a cylindrical tube would seem best. Heating and cooling of the working fluid through the container must also be accommodated. Suitable solutions are shown in outline in Figure 4-9, row 'a'.

A typical commercial catalogue [4.3] shows the following values for round tubes:

Recommended factor of safety: 20 against fracture
Mean tensile fracture strength: 69 MPa
Maximum permissible internal pressure: 690 kPa for 25 mm inside diameter

These values should be compared with the required 5 MPa (see table in step 1.4): a potentially dangerous overload would be imposed, so this alternative and the idea of a flexible container must therefore be rejected.

Flat parallel-sided sight glasses are standardized, and permitted for pressures up to 34 MPa at 40°C, or up to 10 MPa for steam service. Multiple units (two or more lengths of sight glass arranged to show larger fluctuations of liquid levels) for steam boiler application should not be used above 18 MPa at 40°C, 13 MPa at 320°C, or 5.2 MPa in the steam space [4.4]. Using such sight-glasses, volume change by transverse movements of the chamber walls (i.e. across the main axis of the chamber) becomes difficult, because gaskets would need to accommodate sliding movement, and still maintain the seal.

Construction of the container can follow that of some available high pressure sight glass units [4.5]. Overall sizes are approximately 133 × 89 × 390 mm, with a parallel internal section of 304 × 15 × 17 mm. If the total pressure range in step 1.4 is to be

4 – 10

Sight Glass, flat [mm]

$$B = 33.4 \begin{smallmatrix} +0.8 \\ -0.0 \end{smallmatrix}$$

$$T = 17.5 \begin{smallmatrix} +0.0 \\ -0.8 \end{smallmatrix}$$

$$L = 114 \quad 140 \quad 165$$
$$190 \quad 219 \quad 250$$
$$279 \quad 320 \quad 340$$

Gasket

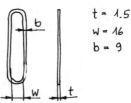

$$t = 1.5$$
$$w = 16$$
$$b = 9$$

covered in this length, the maximum depth of liquid would be limited to 1 mm. Assuming a 5 mm height of liquid would restrict the maximum volume ratio to 61 : 1, allowing densities between 25.8 and 1575 kg/m³, and requiring a minimum working pressure of 500 kPa. The alternative of stacking two sight glasses in series is not considered advantageous, because this would complicate the construction and affect visibility where the frame ends join (a 2 × 19 = 38 mm height).

Based on the above considerations for row 'a' in Figure 4-9, the third variant is chosen. A solid piston would now be difficult to seal adequately, because: (a) the chamber is of rectangular cross-section and corners would cause insurmountable problems; (b) the sight glasses must be sealed to the housing with gaskets, and the tolerances on thickness (between the glasses) will be too large; (c) the working volume must be reducible to zero.

A secondary liquid must be used to transmit pressure from a displacer (the device to solve rows 'c' and 'd' of Figure 4-9) to the working fluid. This also eases the problem of reducing the chamber volume to zero. Thus variant A of the functional structure is required.

Problem 3.3b

The secondary liquid that is needed to transfer the pressure and the motion of the chamber boundary must have a low partial pressure, a high boiling point, and preferably a depressed meniscus edge to enhance visibility of the working fluid. Mercury fulfils these requirements, but needs special materials that are less

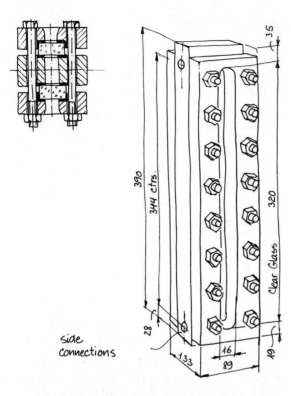

side
connections

susceptible to attack by corrosion or penetration, such as stainless steels. This liquid normally contains dissolved air, and will absorb air until it reaches saturation. Provision must therefore be made to degas the interior of the apparatus and the mercury. This factor should be recorded in the design specification (see Table 4-4).

Problem 3.3c
The next decision concerns putting the working fluid into the chamber, and determining its mass. Lines 'e' and 'f' of the morphological matrix cannot be arbitrarily combined, since there are some incompatibilities.

'Weighing' can be achieved by: (a) the use of a separable pressure container (a 'capsule'), with suitable tubes and valves; (b) weighing of the delivery bottle immediately before and after the fluid transfer operation; or (c) making the experimental chamber detachable to allow direct weighing.

'Calculation' can be performed from 'direct introduction', but can also be performed by introducing the fluid from a capsule. The working fluid in the capsule must be completely displaced into the viewing chamber, therefore the tube connection for such a capsule must be placed below the normal level of the transfer fluid, between the functional blocks

'movement input A' and 'fluid containment C' (see step 2.5).

This apparatus is to be built as a 'one-off', and 'direct introduction' is not at this stage sufficiently well established. For tactical reasons (i.e. creating a line of easy retreat) it is better to make this transfer connection between the functional blocks A and C available as a possible tapping point (e.g. as a tube), to allow attachment of a capsule. Weighing the delivery bottle is likely to be a good check, but not a primary means of measurement of fluid mass. This leads to rejection of the functional groupings '1' and '4' (Figure 4-7).

'Calculation' of the mass of fluid introduced into the chamber depends on the accuracies with which the available quantities can be measured. Best accuracy is expected in the superheated region, with the chamber as full as possible. The table in step 1.4 shows:

500 kPa   30°C   31 kg/m^3

a liquid column of 5 mm height produces a gas column of about 255 mm. Using the estimated chamber cross-section, the expected fill quantity of compound R-13B1 is 6.53×10^{-5} m^3, 2.02 g mass.

Measuring accuracies for major quantities and their errors are:

Temperature, mercury-in-glass thermometer, ± 2°C; at 30°C = 303.15 K the relative error is about 0.67%.
Column height, read directly in the chamber, ± 1 mm; for 255 m height the relative error is about ± 0.40%.
Pressure, Bourdon tube gauge [4.6] calibration accuracy ± 1% of full scale deflection plus one-half of the smallest division interval; for the maximum working pressure selected above, this gauge is delivered with a 6 MPa scale, with 50 kPa divisions, so the estimated error is about ± 85 kPa. At the chosen fill pressure of 500 kPa, the relative error is about $+20$%, -14.5%.

Applying the ideal gas law (pV/t = constant) as a first approximation, the measurement of pressure is critical for the overall accuracy of measuring the mass, and we must expect a total error (the sum of all relative errors) of about $+21$%, -15.5%.

For the filling process, a second pressure gauge with a lower maximum reading could be used, but must be disconnected for normal operation. A suitable gauge would show a maximum reading of 600 kPa, with divisions of 5 kPa. At 500 kPa the resulting relative error is about ± 1.73%. The mass could therefore be calculated to within ± 2.8%.

This total error, and the accuracy with which the mass could be calculated, would be sufficient for the proposed experimental apparatus, and could be improved somewhat in the layout and detail design phases. The effects of using a higher fill pressure and smaller volume should also be investigated to see if this accuracy could be improved. Direct filling of the chamber with the working fluid seems feasible at this stage, but a final decision must be delayed, at least until further design work has been undertaken.

Problem 3.3d
The third decision group concerns the input of motion, the displacer. The alternatives 'Screw and Handwheel' and 'Plunger' appear to be the most favourable. They seem simplest to manufacture, and 'No special provisions' are needed for preventing self-actuated motion, provided that the lead of the screw

is sufficiently small for it to be self-locking. This arrangement is similar to a micrometer screw, and allows a finer sub-division, and more accurate calibration and measurement of the chamber volume. Variant D of the functional structure is thus seen to be optimal. Pressure measurement can be performed either at the fluid chamber of the displacer (variant C) or at the pipeline carrying the secondary liquid.

Problem 3.3e
A further decision concerns setting and controlling the temperature. The whole experimental chamber should ideally be held at a uniform temperature

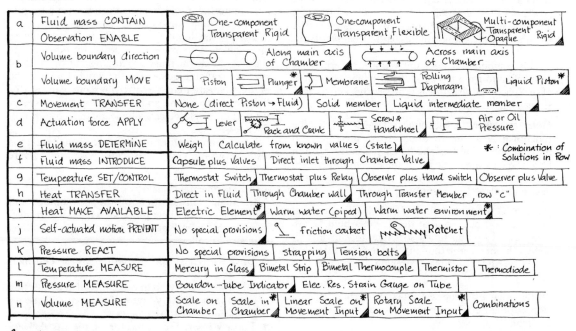

4 – 12

a	Fluid mass CONTAIN / Observation ENABLE	One-component Transparent, Rigid	One-component Transparent, Flexible	Multi-component Transparent Opaque, Rigid		
b	Volume boundary direction	Along main axis of Chamber	Across main axis of Chamber			
	Volume boundary MOVE	Piston	Plunger*	Membrane	Rolling Diaphragm	Liquid Piston*
c	Movement TRANSFER	None (direct Piston → Fluid)	Solid member	Liquid intermediate member		
d	Actuation force APPLY	Lever	Rack and Crank	Screw & Handwheel	Air or Oil Pressure	
e	Fluid mass DETERMINE	Weigh	Calculate from known values (state)		*: Combination of Solutions in Row	
f	Fluid mass INTRODUCE	Capsule plus Valves	Direct inlet through Chamber Valve			
g	Temperature SET/CONTROL	Thermostat Switch	Thermostat plus Relay	Observer plus Hand switch	Observer plus Valve	
h	Heat TRANSFER	Direct in Fluid	Through Chamber wall	Through Transfer Member, row "c"		
i	Heat MAKE AVAILABLE	Electric Element*	Warm water (piped)	Warm water environment*		
j	Self-actuated motion PREVENT	No special provisions	Friction contact	Ratchet		
k	Pressure REACT	No special provisions	Strapping	Tension bolts		
l	Temperature MEASURE	Mercury in Glass	Bimetal Strip	Bimetal Thermocouple	Thermistor	Thermodiode
m	Pressure MEASURE	Bourdon-tube Indicator	Elec. Res. Strain Gauge on Tube			
n	Volume MEASURE	Scale on Chamber	Scale in* Chamber	Linear Scale on* Movement Input	Rotary Scale on* Movement Input	Combinations*

Grouping:
No. ② Fig. 4 – 7

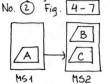

MS1   MS2

Functional Structure:

Main Diagram → Basis, Fig. 4 – 8

Variant	
A	✓
B	✓
C1	✗
C2	✓
D	✓
E	✗
F	✓ plus
G	✓

Concept Sketch:

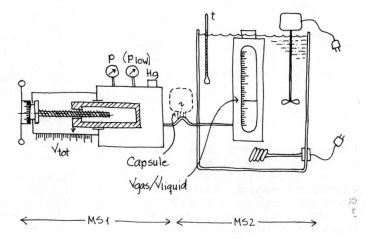

p (P low)   Hg

V_tot

Capsule

V_gas/V_liquid

←——— MS1 ———→ ←——— MS2 ———→

within the working range of 20 to 90°C, without impairing visibility.

Heat can be supplied by: (1) electric current, or (2) hot running water.

Heating the working fluid can be by: (a) heat input to the transfer fluid (mercury), (b) heater on the outside surfaces of the chamber (electric resistance wires or tapes, or water pipe), or (c) immersion of the chamber in hot water.

Control can be achieved by: (i) thermostatic switch, or (ii) thermostatic mixing valve.

The combination (1), (c), (i) appears to be optimal. This combination requires an outer transparent container that can serve as a shield in case the chamber fails. An electric immersion heater with power yet to be determined can be actuated through a thermostatic switch attached to the experimental chamber; water agitation in this bath would be advantageous.

This combination does not require a permanent connection to fixed piping in the building. Variant B of the functional structure is thus selected, and variant E rejected.

Other problems Concerning variant F of the functional structure it would seem preferable to measure the volume of the liquid phase (as column height) on a scale inside the chamber, but to perform the total volume measurement on the motion input device (displacer), as mentioned above.

[Variant G already exists in principle. The internal pressure must be reacted at the chamber boundaries. This part of the functional structure appears at first sight to be an error in thinking, but it draws attention to the need for adequate strength in later design stages.]

Of the originally proposed functional groupings (see step 2.5, Figure 4-7), variant (2) is now recognized as optimal.

3.4 Establish the basic arrangement

Decisions from the previous section are now entered into the clarified morphological matrix (Figure 4-12), together with a sketch of the selected grouping and a concept sketch of the whole apparatus.

3.5 Σ Concepts
Improve   Evaluate, decide   Verify

[In this case study, the investigations of the individual function-carriers contained the cyclic steps of 'elaborating the problem statement', 'searching for solutions', and 'evaluating, deciding', so that the final concept was optimal and completed in steps 3.3 and 3.4. This step has thus been preempted and does not feature in the overall solution.]

Optimal concept

4 Aim: establish the preliminary layouts

4.1 Establish orientation points for form determination

Important aids for this step are sketches, preferably roughly to scale, and proposals for operating instructions. Ergonomic and other data must be used to help the designer towards solutions to the remaining problems.

The general construction of the experimental chamber has been proposed in step 3.3. Connections and means of support are still to be investigated, the most important problem being the means of introducing the working fluid into the chamber.

The motion input device needs to be laid out in more detail with respect to: seals, introducing the transfer fluid (mercury), avoiding air-filled dead spaces, arranging guides for the handwheel and the plunger, positioning the two pressure gauges (for filling and operation), and establishing dimensions of the unit for displacement volume, main diameter, wall thicknesses, etc.

Form-determination for the outer water jacket is also necessary, but does not pose any severe problems.

4.1a Experimental chamber
After some consideration of the possibilities and constraints, the designer proposes a fill-valve arrangement as shown in Figure 4-13, and suggests a filling sequence as follows:

● Open the valve insert so that the lowest 'O'-ring is just above the delivery-bottle connection.
● Displace mercury up into the threaded connection port for the delivery bottle; if necessary release air from the bleed-valve channels.
● Loosely insert the connector of the gas delivery bottle, bleed gas through loose thread to purge air from the delivery pipe, tighten gas connector.
● Retract mercury to the required height as shown on the scale in the chamber; gas flows in under full bottle pressure.
● Close valve insert and disconnect gas bottle connector.
● Adjust column height and gas pressure by slow bleeding of gas through the valve insert, or through a separate fine bleed valve.
● Close and seal the valve insert, plus the gas connection with a sealed screw plug.
● Read measurements, calculate the mass of the working fluid.

4.1b Movement input – plunger displacer
Three basic arrangements may be considered: (a) solid plunger with rising screw spindle; (b) hollow plunger with fixed screw spindle; (c) solid plunger with rising handwheel.

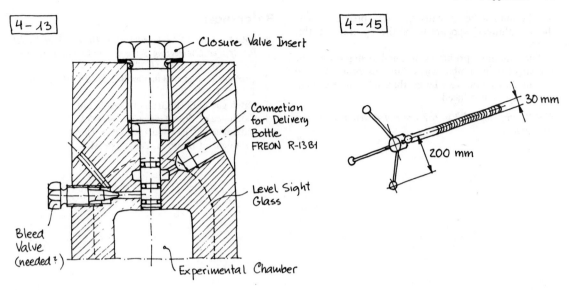

4-13

Closure Valve Insert

Connection for Delivery Bottle FREON R-13B1

Level Sight Glass

Bleed Valve (needed?)

Experimental Chamber

4-15

30 mm

200 mm

4-14

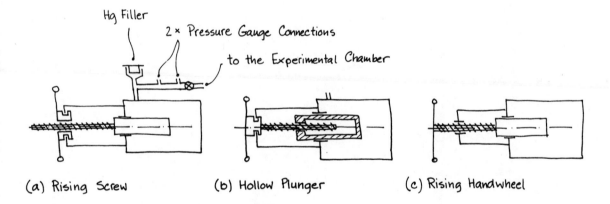

Hg Filler

2 × Pressure Gauge Connections

to the Experimental Chamber

(a) Rising Screw

(b) Hollow Plunger

(c) Rising Handwheel

Displaceable volume must be at least the sum of:

the volume of the experimental chamber
+ the volume of a possible gas transfer capsule
+ the volume of the piping between plunger and chamber
+ the volume of the dead spaces in the measurement and mercury filler connectors

Over-estimation of this chamber volume is not necessarily a disadvantage. Calculation and estimation yields a required volume of about 220 cm³, which is exceeded by a plunger of 50 mm diameter and 120 mm stroke. At the maximum pressure of 5 MPa, the screw is subjected to a force of about 9.8 kN, and requires a core diameter of at least 23 mm to achieve a safety factor of 10 against the 0.2% proof stress of stainless steel (240 MPa). A 30 mm ACME thread with 6 mm lead is satisfactory.

Assuming a friction coefficient of 0.1, and a thrust collar with a mean diameter of 35 mm, the moment required at maximum pressure is about 37 Nm. An adult male can exert a force of 200 N with one hand, and a student about half of that. A crank would need to be about 370 mm long: for two-handed operation this radius can be reduced to about 200 mm. Applying such forces means that the 'rising handwheel' option is not favoured. The disadvantage of the 'rising screw' is that it encroaches into the operating space for the human being, causing safety problems. The 'hollow plunger' appears to be the optimum in this respect.

The remaining problems outlined in step 4.1 can be investigated in similar ways. On this basis, a good preliminary layout can be established, and a dimensional layout produced.

Concluding steps 4.2 to 6.7 are not developed for this case study.

References

1. BOLZ R.E. and TUVE, G.L. (eds), *CRC Handbook of Tables for Applied Engineering Science*, The Chemical Rubber Co., Cleveland, Ohio (1970)
2. DuPont Technical Bulletins B-2, B-12A, B-12B, S-16, T-13A, T-13B, RT-32
3. Catalogue of QVF Glass of Canada Ltd.
4. Catalogue of Ernst Gage Co., NJ, USA
5. Catalogue of Clark-Reliance, Ohio, USA
6. Catalogue of Bourdon, Paris, type MIX

Case 5 Punched tape winder

A hand-operated winder for punched computer tape is likely to be a fairly simple technical system, and could be underestimated as a technical problem. The design process for this device is, however, very illustrative because all the required design characteristics for this system allow the designer to generate alternatives in almost all phases of the design process. The complexity of the device and its design difficulty are sufficiently low to encourage a continuous overview of the sequence used in the design process (Figure 5-1).

Introduction

A large manufacturer of mechanical engineering equipment needs a number of hand-operated winders for punched computer tape to satisfy in-house requirements. As they have spare capacity in their workshops (particularly the toolroom) they decide to investigate designing and manufacturing these devices using their own facilities. The problem, as formulated by the potential users, is shown in Figure 5-2, and is assigned to the design department with instructions to produce the necessary layouts, detail and assembly drawings using a systematic design procedure.

Problem assignment

1 Aim: elaborate or clarify the assigned specification

1.1 Critically recognize the assigned problem

1.2 Establish the state of the art

1.3 Analyse the problem situation

1.4 Examine the possibilities of realization

Comments refer to combined use of steps 1.1 to 1.4.

The design team meets to discuss this problem, and pictures or advertising leaflets of existing tape winders are examined to establish the state of the art. There is no hesitation in recognizing that such a device is feasible (step 1.4).

1.5 Complete the requirements, classify and quantify, set priorities

1.6 Work out the full design specification (list of requirements)

Comments refer to combined use of steps 1.5 and 1.6.

A small group is selected to work out a full design

specification as a prerequisite to using further systematic procedures. They start their work from the assigned specification and the results of the preceding discussions. A guideline for the classifications to be used is obtained from a published survey of classes of properties (*Principles*, Figure 5). After checking and review by management, the design specification as shown in Figure 5-3 is accepted as the 'contract' for the design team.

1.7 Prepare and plan for problem-solving

In order to co-ordinate the work of the design groups, a plan for exchanging opinions, results and advice after each of steps 2.7, 3.5, 4.6, and 5.6 is agreed. These progress conferences provide opportunities to perform evaluations, to optimize results, and to release the approved solutions as bases for the subsequent steps in the design process.

Design specification

2 Aim: establish the functional structures

2.1 Abstract: produce the black box representations

In the first step of this sequence, a 'black box' diagram of the process (as shown in Figure 5-4) is sketched. It represents the transformation of the punched tape (the operand) from a loose stack (state 1) into a properly wound roll (state 2).

2.2 Establish the technological principles
Establish the sequences of operations

The transformation 'winding tape to a roll' can be accomplished in three ways, as shown in Figure 5-5. Consequently, three variants for the technology of winding tapes are available. Considering that the operand (the punched tape) must not be damaged by the winding process, the variant 'rotating mandrel' seems to be most useful and is selected for consideration in the subsequent design steps.

2.3 Establish the technical process,
TP → optimal TP

A complete sequence of operations is described based on the general model of the structure of a process (*Principles*, Figure 2.) This ensures that the desired

Figure 5-1

Steps from General Model according to Figure 0.1	Step	Progress of case	Design documents
1 Aim: elaborate or clarify the assigned specification	1.1 1.2 1.3 1.4 1.5 1.6 1.7	Problem Assignment 5-2 5-3	Design Specification
2 Aim: establish the functional structures	2.1 2.2 2.3 2.4 2.5 2.6 2.7	5-4 5-5 5-6 5-7 5-8	Black Box Technology Technical Process Functional Structure
3 Aim: establish the concepts	3.1 3.2 3.3 3.4 3.5	5-9 5-10 5-11 5-12 5-13 5-14 5-15 5-16 5-17	Morphological Matrix Arrangement Matrix Concept Sketches Evaluation
4 Aim: establish the preliminary layouts	4.1 4.2 4.3 4.4 4.5 4.6	5-18 5-19 5-20 5-21	Preliminary Layouts Evaluation
5 Aim: establish the dimensional layouts	5.1 5.2 5.3 5.4 5.5 5.6	5-22 5-23	Dimensional Layouts
6 Aim: detailing, elaboration	6.1 6.2 6.3 6.4 6.5 6.6 6.7		

Figure 5-2 Problem assignment — design contract as agreed between the design team and management
Problem situation The punched data tape from a computer-driven tape punch unit is usually caught in an open box, loosely and randomly coiled or looped. For storage, and insertion into a tape reader, the tape must be wound into an even roll. The winding operation is usually performed using a tape winder, which is generally hand driven and fastened to the edge of a table.
The tape winders currently on the market are considered to be relatively expensive.
Task Design a tape winder.
Data and conditions Tape width $w = 25$ mm Diameter of hollow core in centre of tape roll $d = 25$ mm Maximum outside diameter of wound tape roll $D_{max} = 195$ mm The tape should be held lightly on a core-former to start winding. The finished roll should be easily removable from the core-former using a minimum of force, so that none of the windings of the roll are laterally displaced during removal. (Note: it is assumed that the duty of attaching the correct end of the tape to the winder is the operator's responsibility, so no provisions for checking this condition are to be incorporated.) Hand drive, if possible with mechanical advantage to increase speed. Both rotational directions. Fastening of device to the table without use of tools. Small batch to be produced. Price of comparable devices on the market about SwFr 500.

transformation can be achieved with the selected technology. The resulting diagram that summarizes this technical process is shown in Figure 5-6.

In addition to the main process that transforms the operand (the punched tape), the diagram of the technical process also contains the 'preparation' and 'conclusion' operations (in the dashed boxes) that need to be performed either by the technical system or by the human operator in order to use the device. In examining these operations the designer tries to perceive any additional functions that the tape winder must perform and, consequently, tries to add to the list of requirements for the device. The functions of

the main device are not active for these added functions, but the winder must be able (passively) to accept operations performed on it, e.g. 'Connection with the table: PERMIT'.

2.4 Apply technical systems to the process, and establish boundaries

The tasks of forming the 'mandrel', and rotating it (using energy delivered by the human being through the hand drive) is allocated to the technical system (Figure 5-7). Grasping the tape end, and removing the finished roll of tape, are recognized as two functions of the technical system for which the device must provide the necessary conditions for the task to be performed by the human operator. The TS is thus 'passive', in the same sense as for the 'connection to the table' mentioned in the previous step. The verb 'ENABLE' indicates the special character of this function: it cannot be realized by the technical system alone, but only if aided by the human operator. The additional function of aligning the tape correctly, 'Tape for winding: GUIDE', is considered to be a desirable function, not a fixed requirement.

2.5 Establish the groupings of functions

In this case, there is no question about grouping any functions. Any aggregations or separation is seen to be subject to obvious disadvantages. Grouping of functions is likely to obscure some of the functional needs without revealing alternative solutions, and further sub-division of functions is unlikely to improve the process of solving this problem.

2.6 Establish the functional structures, and represent them

Based on the decisions reached in step 2.4, a functional structure can be generated. The only variant indicated in this functional structure is the partial function 8: 'Punched tape for winding: GUIDE', which has already been mentioned in step 2.4 as being desirable but not essential.

A functional structure can be represented in the form of a function tree (figure 5-7), or a block schematic (Figure 5-8), but only the latter can show both the partial functions and their relationships as demanded by the definition of the term 'structure' (*Principles*, Glossary item 43). The contents, in terms of the partial functions, are otherwise identical, and describe the active and passive capabilities allocated to the system to be designed.

The purpose of placing the word 'mandrel' in quotation marks is to avoid making this function-carrier too concrete early in the design sequence. The action location for forming the central hollow core of the roll may or may not be a full pin-shaped item. Step 3 in this design procedure explains the implications.

Figure 5-3   Clarified design specification

	Fixed req.	Desire
1 Function Winding punched computer tapes into rolls	*	
2 Functionally determined properties 2.1 Tape dimensions: width 25 mm thickness 0.5 mm Material: paper, tear strength 50 N	*	
2.2 Roll dimensions: inside dia. 25 mm max. outside dia. 195 mm	*	
Tolerances: flatness: sideways offset from layer to layer 0.1 mm max., total cone height on one side 3 mm max. Mass: 300 g max.		*
2.3 Fastening: screwed for constant use		*
clamped for occasional use Table: office table, wood, top 30 mm max. thick		*
2.4 Process of winding: Tension on tape 25 N Max.	*	
Winding speed 2 m/s max.	*	
Indication of diameter of wound roll		*
Winding in either direction	*	
Fastening of tape end with one hand		*
Non-return, no unwinding of roll by loosely hanging tape	*	
No free-wheeling (danger of edge damage)	*	
Braking facility (no free-wheeling, and tape must not be broken during winding, see reference to tear strength above)		*
Same rotation direction for drive mechanism and winding of roll		*
Easy removal of roll	*	
2.5 Environment: office with usual climatic conditions	*	
3 Operational properties Life: 2500 hours (about 7.5×10^6 revolutions)	*	
Maintenance-free		*
Easy repair by non-technical staff		*
Shock resistant: free fall on concrete surface from 1 m		*
4 Ergonomic properties Hand drive: force 10–20 N, speed 0.5 m/s	*	
Safety against operator injury (stability of device, no trapping points for hands or fingers)	*	
Low noise	*	
Non-staining	*	
Suitable for right- or left-handed persons		*
5 Appearance Similar to usual data processing equipment		*
6 Transport Easy transportability (carrying by female operator)	*	
Small storage volume		*
7 Delivery properties Small batch, about 50 off	*	
Delivery deadline 1 year	*	
8 Economic properties Aim: manufacturing cost about SwFr 100 (price of competing product about SwFr 500)	*	

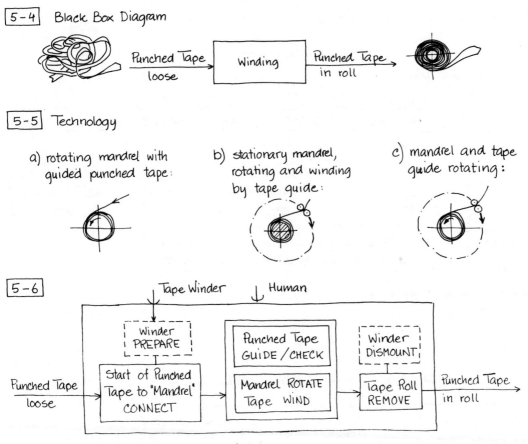

5-4 Black Box Diagram

Punched Tape loose → [Winding] → Punched Tape in roll

5-5 Technology

a) rotating mandrel with guided punched tape:

b) stationary mandrel, rotating and winding by tape guide:

c) mandrel and tape guide rotating:

5-6

Tape Winder ↓   Human ↓

Punched Tape loose →

| Winder PREPARE |

Start of Punched Tape to "Mandrel" CONNECT →

Punched Tape GUIDE / CHECK

Mandrel ROTATE Tape WIND →

| Winder DISMOUNT |

Tape Roll REMOVE → Punched Tape in roll

"Mandrel" = central body, former

2.7 Σ Functional structures
Improve Evaluate, decide Verify

Optimal functional structure

3 Aim: establish the concepts

3.1 Establish the inputs and modes of action

The only significant input to the device defined by the designer is the motion and energy provided manually. This motion is to be transformed into the rotational motion of the 'mandrel' by the action of the device. This description therefore indicates the duties that the action chain within the device has to perform.

3.2 Establish the classes of function-carrier (morphological matrix)

A search to find classes of function-carrier for each of the partial functions shown in the functional structure is conducted. Examining different action principles, as shown in the morphological matrix, Figure 5-9, is a useful aid. The function-carriers shown for function 2 now demonstrate why the idea of a solid mandrel should not have become fixed into the conceptual picture since the 'mandrel' can also be formed as an envelope of contact points which form the tape end into a cylindrical hollow core.

3.3 Combine the function-carriers, examine their relationships

In order to work out the concepts, the function-carriers must first be combined in as many ways as possible, and their compatibility tested. In this case, the designer is free to combine three different organs:

● the 'mandrel' as action location for connecting the punched tape to the device, functions 1, 2, 6, 7, and 9
● the organs for accepting, transforming and transmitting energy, functions 4 and 5
● the organ for connecting the device to the table, function 10

5-7   Functional Structure – hierarchical tree

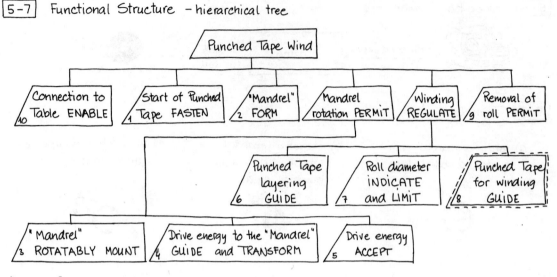

"Mandrel" = central body, former

5-8   Functional Structure – Block Schematic with Relationships

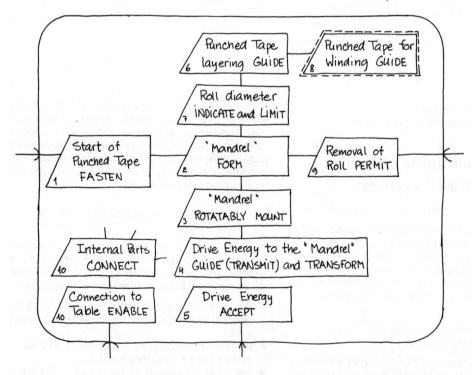

5-9 Morphological Matrix

	FUNCTIONS:		ACTION PRINCIPLES (AP) / FUNCTION CARRIERS (FC) :
1	Start of Punched Tape FASTEN	AP	Direct connection of tape to "mandrel" — Mechanical: Force-locking [Form-locking, Friction, Clip/Clamp], Material-locking [permant, tempor'y], Pneumatic: — Indirect Connection:
		FC	Pin; N; Glue Tape; Tape thread
2	"Mandrel" FORM	AP	Cont. surface (no gaps) — Discontinuous surface (cylindrical envelope) [cylindrical, full body, part body]
		FC	
3	"Mandrel" ROTATIONALLY MOUNT Bearing types: radial/axial	AP	Sliding bearing — Dry and mixed lubrication / Liquid or gas lub. — Rolling bearing — Magnetic bearing
		FC	Self-lub. / Grease-lub. / Oil-lub. / Solids as lub. / hydro-dynamic / hydro-static / Ball, Needle, Taper-roller, Parallel-roller, Barrel-roller
4	Drive energy to the "mandrel" GUIDE (TRANSMIT) and TRANSFORM	AP	Mechanical: Form-closure — Force-closure (Friction drive) — Hydraulic: [hydro-dyn., hydro-static] — Electrical: Generator/Motor
		FC	Gear wheels / chain / Tooth belt / Vee-belt / Round belt / Flat belt / Friction wheel
5	Drive energy ACCEPT	AP	Mechanical Transmissions: Rotary movement: — Translational movement:
		FC	Crank; Wheel Handle; Lever; Rack/Pinion; String/rope
6	Punched Tape layering GUIDE	AP	One side flange: [full surface, partial surf.] — Two side flanges [full surface, partial surf, fix distance, variable distance]
7	Roll diameter INDICATE and LIMIT	AP	Direct: measure diameter: [Ruler scale, Mechanical feeler, Optical feeler] — Indirect: measure other values [Movement]
		FC	Scale on side flange / Feeler (pin) / Photo-cell / Revolution counter / Length measurem.
8	Punched Tape for winding GUIDE	AP	Mechanical guidance — By hand
		FC	open eye: / angled entry: / pre-pos. roller with flanges:
9	Removal of roll PERMIT	AP	Friction to "mandrel" reduce: / Axial force applied to inner diameter: / Mandrel diameter reduce:
		FC	air
10	Connection to Table ENABLE	AP	Mechanical: Force-locking / Force and Form-locking / Form-locking — Magnetic — Pneumatic
		FC	Self-weight / / screws

5-10   Arrangement Matrix

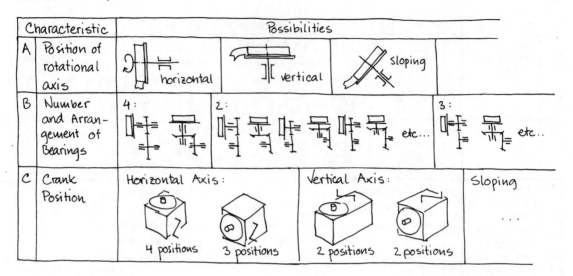

Characteristic	Possibilities			
A Position of rotational axis	horizontal	vertical	sloping	
B Number and Arrangement of Bearings	4:	2: ... etc...	3: ... etc...	
C Crank Position	Horizontal Axis: 4 positions 3 positions		Vertical Axis: 2 positions 2 positions	Sloping ...

The fact that all function-carriers in one of these groups are mutually compatible with any function-carriers in the other two groups permits an independent optimization within each group of functions, simplifying the overall optimization.

Possibilities for the spatial arrangement of the transmission functions can also be analysed. Figure 5-10 shows these possibilities in a matrix, based on characteristics A to C of such a drive.

3.4   Establish the basic arrangements

The two matrix diagrams, Figures 5-9 and 5-10, contain a large number of proposed solutions. In this step the designer synthesizes a number of such solutions. A rough assessment of the available possibilities leads to selecting the concepts shown in Figures 5-11 to 5-16. Some of the variants allow less scope for alternative solutions, but the variety of possibilities is increased by the mutual compatibility of solutions, and this provides the ability to combine the three groups mentioned in step 3.3 without constraints.

3.5   Σ Concepts
Improve. Evaluate, decide   Verify

Figure 5-17 shows a coarse evaluation based on the selected criteria of usage and expenditure, using only (+) or (−) to differentiate solutions. All solution variants use a hand crank. The assessment for the 'drive transmission' favours a chain or a belt with round cross-section. For the 'mandrel' the highest assessment is obtained for a solid mandrel (less than 25 mm long) with slots, or an arrangement of four pins (variant 4). Evaluating the 'transmission costs' is

helped by price estimates being available for the different drive arrangements. Bearing costs are estimated from experience, using an average price and the number of bearings. The housing costs are based on its shape, machining requirements and likely complexity.

Optimal Concept

4   Aim: establish the preliminary layouts

4.1   Establish the orientation points for form determination

4.2   Establish the arrangements, investigate re-use, rough form-giving, partial dimensioning

4.3   Establish the types of material, classes of manufacturing method, tolerances and surface properties where necessary

4.4   Investigate the critical form-determination zones

Steps 4.1 to 4.4 are omitted for this case.

4.5   Represent the preliminary layouts

The preliminary layouts are executed as freehand sketches, roughly to scale. They can be used to investigate those function-carriers that have already been established, and the many regions where different manufacturing methods could influence the forms of components. Variant 3 resulting from this investigation yields a complicated item to fulfil the function 'Connection with the table: ENABLE'. It could

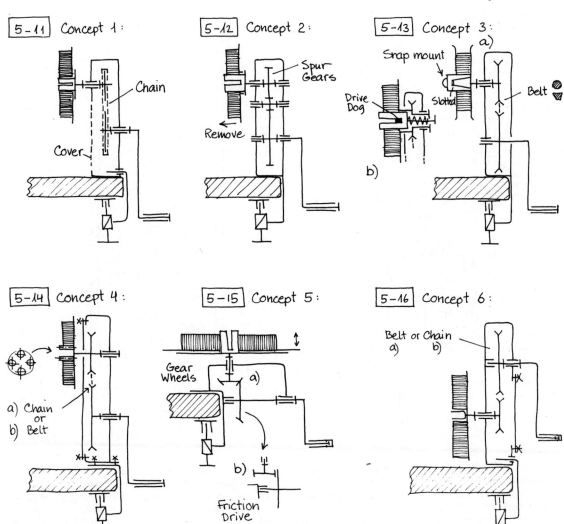

5-11 Concept 1:

Chain
Cover

5-12 Concept 2:

Spur Gears
Remove

5-13 Concept 3:
a)
Snap mount
Drive Dog
Slotted
Belt
b)

5-14 Concept 4:

a) Chain or
b) Belt

5-15 Concept 5:

Gear Wheels
a)
b)
Friction Drive

5-16 Concept 6:

Belt or Chain
a)   b)

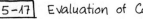

5-17 Evaluation of Concepts:

USAGE

Criterion/Properties	1	2	3a	3b	4a	4b	5a	5b	6a	6b
1 Tape End HOLD	+	+	−	+	+	+	+	+	+	+
2 Coiling/Handling	+	+	+	+	+	+	±	±	+	+
3 TapeCoil REMOVE	±	+	+	+	+	+	+	+	+	+
4 Life – Servicing	+	+	±	±	+	+	+	−	±	+
5										
6										
Sum	3.5	4	2.5	3.5	4	4	3.5	2.5	3.5	4

EXPENDITURE

Criterion/Properties	1	2	3a	3b	4a	4b	5a	5b	6a	6b
1 Drive Costs	+	−	±	±	+	+	±	+	±	+
2 Bearing Costs	+	−	+	+	+	+	±	±	±	±
3 Housing Costs	+	−	+	+	+	+	±	±	±	±
4										
5										
6										
Sum	3	−	2.5	2.5	3	3	1.5	2.0	1.5	2.0

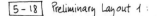

5-18   Preliminary Layout 1 :

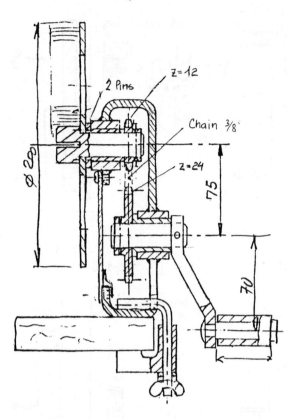

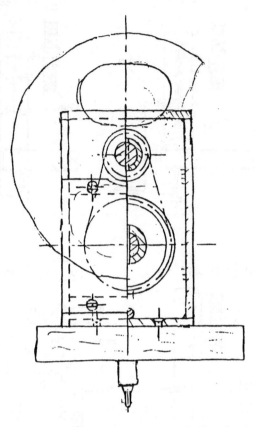

possibly be used to fasten other devices to the table. Variant 2 solves the desired function 8 'Punched tape for winding: GUIDE' by means of a flanged guide roller that can be fixed to the housing. This would enable the operator to align the tape more easily, and can be used with either winding direction (and it is therefore suitable for either right-handed or left-handed operation).

These preliminary layouts are represented in Figures 5-18 to 5-20.

4.6   Σ Preliminary layout
   Improve   Evaluate, decide   Verify

This evaluation is performed using point rating and a relative strength diagram (Figure 5-21). The designer at first selects six criteria for usage value to judge the proposals, and calculates the sum and relative technical value. Reviewing this chart, the designer now notices that two criteria (4 and 6) have received the same values for all variants. These criteria are obviously not contributing to the evaluation, and are consequently eliminated. Recalculating produces the revised sum. The resulting numbers in the original and revised sums show the influence of the number of

criteria. The relative values would have been appreciably higher if the criteria with identical evaluations had remained in the assessment, making discrimination between the variants more difficult. The manufacturing and assembly costs are estimated and also used to assess the proposed solutions.

The relative strength diagram shows the position of each solution. The expenditure values are still capable of improvement, which is the reason for deferring a decision between these solutions until the dimensional layouts have been established.

Optimum preliminary layout

5   Aim: establish the dimensional layouts

5.1   Deliver the substantiation for certain design characteristics

The design calculations are not shown. They typically cover such items as the selection of belt cross-section, pulley diameters, pulley centre distances (to produce controlled stretch of the belt and traction forces within acceptable limits), etc.

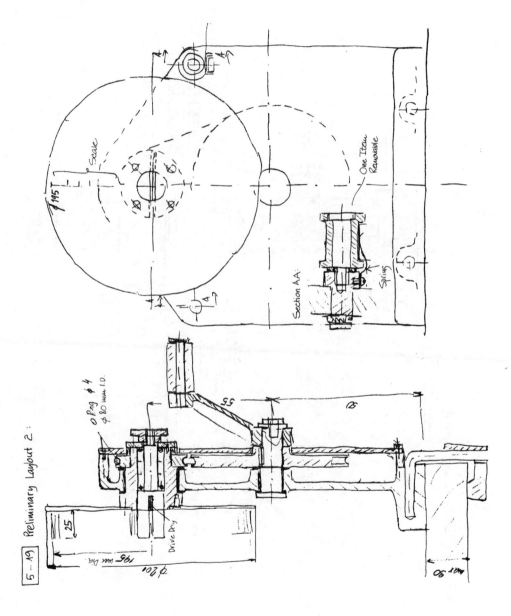

5 – 19   Preliminary Layout 2:

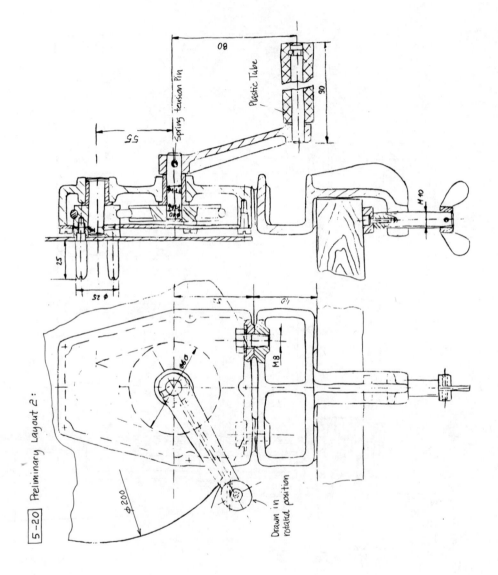

5-20 Preliminary Layout 2:

| 5 - 21 | Evaluation of Preliminary Layouts

USAGE

Criterion:	Ideal	1'	2'	3'
1	Time for Rolling/Removal	4	3	4	4
2	Tape Guidance at Entry	4	2	4	2
3	Fixing to table (handling/safety)	4	3	3	4
4	Transport and Storage	4	4	4	4
5	Life, Maintenance	4	4	3	3
6	Safety	4	4	4	4
	Sum	24	20	22	21
	Techn. Relative Value	1	0.83	0.92	0.88
	Revised sum*	16	12	14	13
	Revised Techn. Relative Value	1	0.75	0.88	0.81

EXPENDITURE

Criterion:	Ideal	1'	2'	3'
1	Manuf. Costs : Drive and Bearings	4	3	4	4
2	Manuf. Costs : Housing (incl. Tape Guide and Table Mount)	4	4	2	3
3	Assembly Costs	4	3	3	4
4					
5					
6					
	Sum	12	10	9	11
	Expenditure Rel. Value	1	0.83	0.75	0.92

* Two "equal" evaluations removed

Relative Strength Diagram:

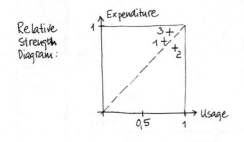

Points scores for Evaluation:

4 Very good
3 good
2 acceptable
1 deficient
0 unusable

5.2 Establish the definitive arrangement, form determination, partial dimensioning

5.3 Establish the definitive and complete determination of materials, manufacturing methods, partial definitive determination of tolerances and surface properties

5.4 Optimize the critical form determination zones

5.5 Represent the dimensional layouts

Comments refer to combined use of steps 5.2 to 5.5.

Figures 5-22 and 5-23 show two variants as dimensional layouts. Comparison with the preliminary layouts shows differences, particularly with respect to the amount and detail of the information contained in these representations. these layouts permit the designer to obtain good estimates of manufacturing costs.

Concluding steps 5.6 to 6.7 are not developed for this case.

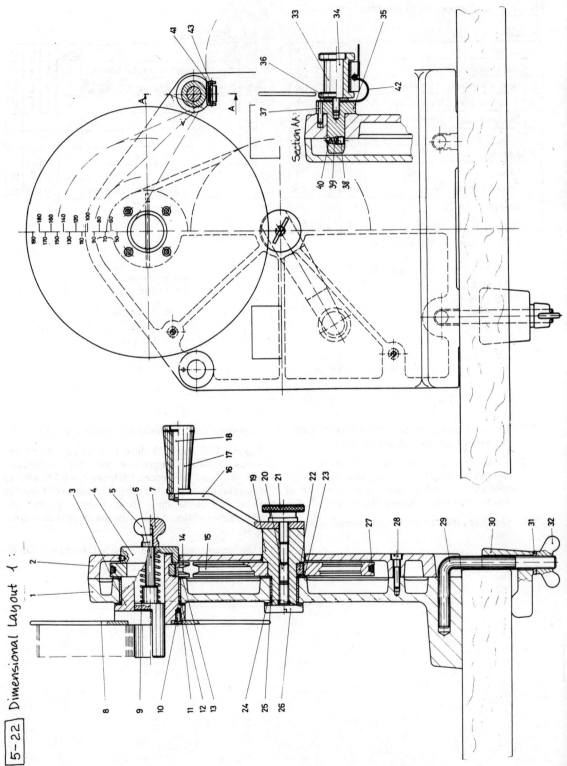

Section AA

Dimensional Layout 1 :

5-22

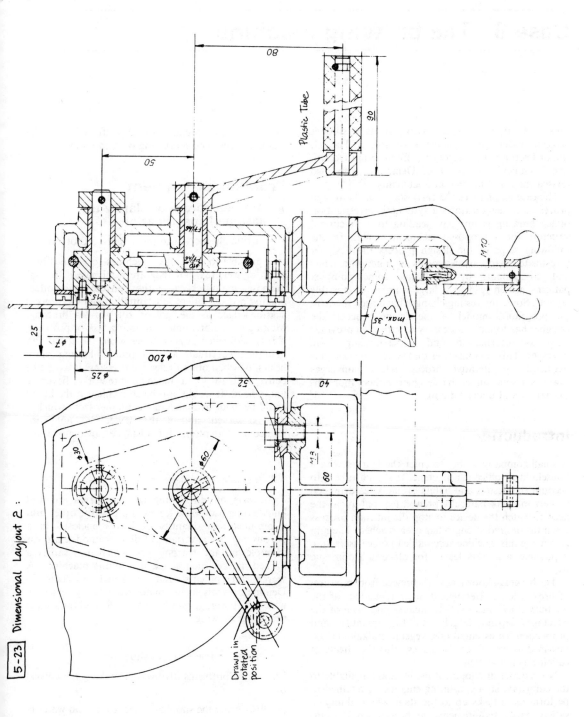

5-23 Dimensional Layout 2:

Case 6 Tea brewing machine

This case originated some years ago as a student project, under the supervision of Eskild Tjalve*, Senior Lecturer, Laboratory for Engineering Design, The Technical University of Denmark, who also revised the resulting project documents.

The case emphasizes the early stages of the design process, and demonstrates a systematic investigation of tea brewing technology, leading to a functional structure for a proposed technical system. In the following steps of the design process the designer investigates many arrangements of function-carriers and components by producing some complex patterns, which lead to a large number of possible layouts. Some interesting changes have been made in the procedural model of the design process: the designer has found it necessary to return to previous steps as information and understanding have increased. This demonstrates that systematic design is frequently an iterative process which converges towards a solution as the designer gathers more information and understanding.

Introduction

A small company wishes to enter the market with a household or office tea machine. It should take into account the desires and habits of many tea drinkers, namely to drink naturally brewed tea, but avoid the need to watch the device to stop the infusion process when the desired strength has been reached. The aim is to make this machine acceptable to office users and, if possible, a market leader for office and domestic use.

The beverage known as tea is brewed from mixtures of broken leaves (fermented or unfermented) of the tea bush (*thea sinensis*). The quality and taste of the beverage depend largely on the quantity and proportions of essential oils, vegetable alkaloids and tannin dissolved from the leaves, plus the effects of caffeine as a stimulant.

No product development facilities are available to the company, so a consulting engineer is retained to perform these tasks up to the stage where ability to satisfy market requirements can be assessed. It seems

*We gratefully acknowledge permission from Dr Tjalve to reproduce the drawings, and to adapt the text of his work.

likely that the company can successfully handle the manufacturing and marketing of such a device.

Problem assignment

1 Aim: elaborate or clarify the assigned specification

1.1 Critically recognize the assigned problem

It is possible to use coffee machines to make (brew, mash or wet) tea, but they are rarely used for that purpose, mainly because the conventional coffee-making process differs substantially from the process acknowledged as the 'golden rule' of tea brewing. Making tea is not a time-consuming task or problem, if it is performed at such times when the social and manipulative rituals are acceptable. During office hours, or when other duties are pressing, it would be convenient to let a machine brew the beverage unattended. It would also be convenient if the liquid could be made available in a container from which it can be served, and if the device did not need immediate attention, for instance to remove tea leaves.

1.2 Establish the state of the art

Two ways of introducing the tea leaves are well known; one uses loose leaves in a pot, the other uses a pre-measured quantity of leaves enclosed in a porous bag. Some variants of these methods exist, for example 'instant' tea powders, which may satisfy a limited market such as use in vending machines. A search for patents and marketed products in Denmark reveals no automated tea brewing devices in which the beverage may be left unattended for a short time after brewing.

1.3 Analyse the problem situation

The major problems involved in making tea consist of:

(a) dispensing the supplies of tea leaves and water in correct proportions;
(b) establishing the right conditions for extracting the tea constituents from the leaves;
(c) regulating the extraction time by interrupting the contact between the infused beverage and the tea

Figure 6-1

Steps from General Model according to Figure 0.1	Step	Progress of case	Design documents
1 Aim: elaborate or clarify the assigned specification	1.1 1.2 1.3 1.4 1.5 1.6 1.7	Problem Assignment 6-2	Evaluation Criteria
2 Aim: establish the functional structures	2.1 2.2 2.3 2.4 2.5 2.6 2.7	6-3 6-4 6-6-7-8-9-10 6-15 6-5 6-14 6-11	Black Box Technological Principles Technical Process Functional Structure
3 Aim: establish the concepts	3.1 3.2 3.3 3.4 3.5	6-12 6-13 6-19 6-16,-17-18 6-20 6-21-22,-23-24	Concepts Basic Arrangements Preliminary Layouts Improvement and Evaluation Orientation Points
4 Aim: establish the preliminary layouts	4.1 4.2 4.3 4.4 4.5 4.6	6-25 6-26 6-27 6-28 6-29 6-30 6-31	Detail Arrangements Form Determination and Prototype
5 Aim: establish the dimensional layouts	5.1 5.2 5.3 5.4 5.5 5.6		
6 Aim: detailing, elaboration	6.1 6.2 6.3 6.4 6.5 6.6 6.7		

leaves after a suitable and adjustable period of time.

1.4   Examine the possibilities of realization

It seems that there are no basic technical obstacles to creating a tea machine, but at this stage it is doubtful whether an economical and operationally acceptable solution can be found. The purpose of the following work is to try to remove this element of doubt, showing that a tea machine is feasible by actually designing a tea machine.

1.5   Complete the requirements, classify and quantify, set priorities

The task may be formulated as follows: 'Design a machine system for automatic brewing of tea from commercially available leaves, primarily for use in small offices or the home'. Additional conditions and constraints are as follows. *Inputs*: cold water, tea leaves in appropriate amounts, electrical energy, information about extraction time. *Outputs*: hot tea, separated leaf remains, both to be removed in a suitable manner from the device.

1.6   Work out the full design specification (list of requirements)

The task of designing this tea machine is performed by one person. As an aid to later evaluation of the proposals the designer sets up a chart of weighting and rating points, with descriptions of the criteria to use at appropriate stages of work (Figure 6-2). Further revision of the above statements into a design specification following the formalized approach used in other cases in this book is not considered particularly useful at this stage.

1.7   Prepare and plan for problem-solving

Limitations on time to complete this project have not been set, but a number of points in the design process at which decisions about continuing the project can be taken are proposed. Consultations are planned in steps 2.7, 3.5, 4.6, 5.6 and 6.7, particularly when some costs can be estimated, after modelling, detailing, and tool design.

Design specification

2   Aim: establish the functional structures

2.1   Abstract: produce the black box representations

The desired process (the transformation as expressed in the problem formulation) is shown as a 'black box' process in Figure 6-3.

2.2   Establish the technological principles Establish the sequence of operations

Two important partial processes for tea brewing are 'heating', and 'extracting the tea substances' from the leaves. Technological principles for these partial processes are shown in Figure 6-4. Heating can be realized by supplying electrical energy as input, and transferring heat by conduction and convection from a heating element directly to the liquid. The partial process of extracting the tea substances may be provided (1) by immersing tea leaves in hot (preferably boiling) water for a suitable time period, or (2) by letting the water stay in contact with the tea leaves for a suitable duration in a flow process (similar to one of the usual coffee processes). (3) An alter-

---

| 6-2 | Allocation of Weights to Properties, and Rating Points to Solution Qualities:

Property:	Weight:	Rating points: 1	2	3	4	5
Easy to operate (incl. cleaning)	5	Two operations needed (such as using a coffeemachine for tea)	One complicated operation + difficult to clean	One complicated operation + easy to clean	One easy operation + difficult to clean	One easy operation + easy to clean
Low price	5	> 200 Dkr.	200 – 175	175 – 150	150 – 125	125 >
Small space	3	> 4 × T	> 3 × T	> 2½ × T	> 2 × T	< 2 × T
		where T = the volume of a serving container				
Reliable function	4	Very poor	—	—	—	Very good
Good appearance	4	Very poor	—	—	—	Very good

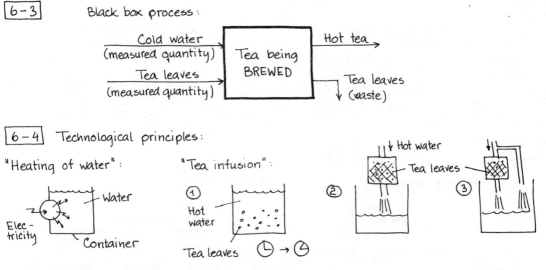

6-3   Black box process:

Cold water (measured quantity) → | Tea being BREWED | → Hot tea
Tea leaves (measured quantity) →   → Tea leaves (waste)

6-4   Technological principles:

"Heating of water":   "Tea infusion":

Water · Container · Electricity

① Hot water · Tea leaves 🕐 → 🕓

② Hot water · Tea leaves

③

native to (2) could be to allow only a part of the water flow to contact the leaves. Contact between the water and the tea leaves should cease after the appropriate brewing time.

2.3   Establish the technical processes, TP → optimal TP

These considerations about processes lead to three different process structures (Figure 6-5). The designer decides to investigate tea brewing by means of a flow process based on the alternative shown in Figure 6-5(a).

The designer takes a closer look at the technological principles for each of the sub-processes.

Heating the water by direct heat transfer needs two steps: (a) forming a hot surface (as the 'tool surface' for the technology), and (b) bringing the hot surface and the water into good thermal contact. Possibilities for performing this operation are shown in Figure 6-6.

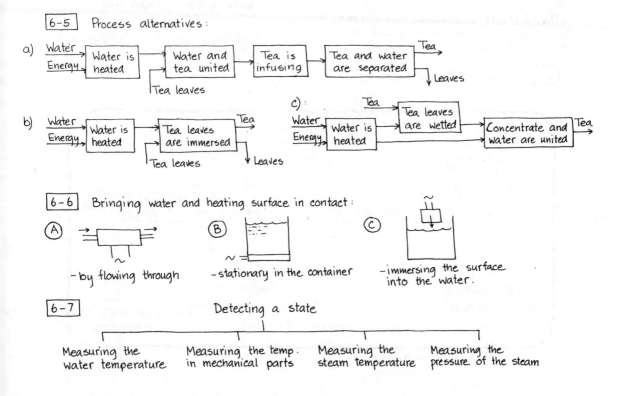

6-5   Process alternatives:

a) Water, Energy → Water is heated → Water and tea united ← Tea leaves → Tea is infusing → Tea and water are separated → Tea / Leaves

b) Water, Energy → Water is heated → Tea leaves are immersed ← Tea leaves → Tea / ↓ Leaves

c): Water, Energy → Water is heated → Tea leaves are wetted → Tea / Concentrate and water are united → Tea

6-6   Bringing water and heating surface in contact:

Ⓐ – by flowing through   Ⓑ – stationary in the container   Ⓒ – immersing the surface into the water.

6-7   Detecting a state

Measuring the water temperature | Measuring the temp. in mechanical parts | Measuring the steam temperature | Measuring the pressure of the steam

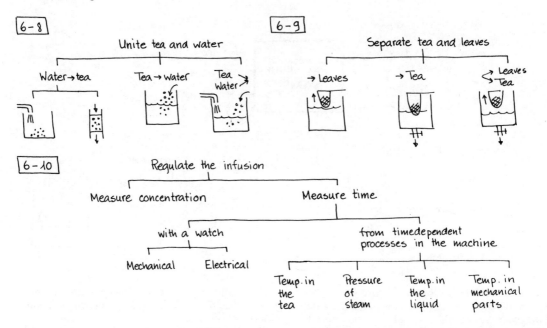

It is also necessary to provide thermal control (especially for variants B and C), by detecting a suitable variable (Figure 6-7) and hence regulating the input energy either continuously or by a two-state (on-off or bang-bang) control.

The sub-process of *uniting tea leaves and water* may be performed in a number of ways, as shown in Figure 6-8.

The sub-process of *separating tea leaves from the liquid* may be accomplished by one of the means shown in Figure 6-9.

The sub-process of *allowing the tea to brew* is passive, i.e. it needs no positive action but proceeds by itself while the water is in contact with the tea leaves. Control is needed to terminate the process. A suitable variable must be detected to determine the end of the desired brewing period, and to start the process of 'separating tea leaves from the liquid'. Some suitable principles are outlined in Figure 6-10.

2.4   Apply technical systems to the process and establish boundaries

6-11   Functional structure:

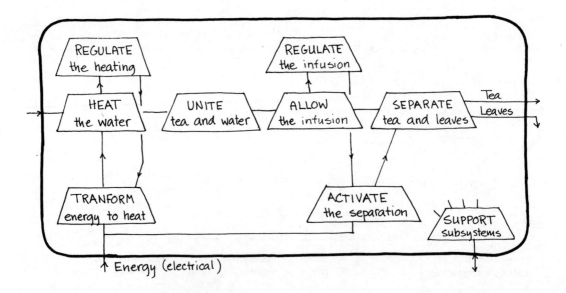

2.5   Establish the groupings of functions

2.6   Establish the functional structures, and represent them

Comments refer to combined use of steps 2.4 to 2.6.

At this stage the designer decides to try to solve all control functions electrically, and produces a functional structure as shown in Figure 6-11. This is neither the only functional structure possible, nor is it general for all tea machines. Many of the decisions taken about technological principles and types of input have influenced the form of this particular structure.

2.7   Σ Functional structures
      Improve   Evaluate, decide   Verify

Optimal functional structure

3   Aim: establish the concepts

In this case, the designer decides to use a stepwise progression to establish the concept, by incorporating one function after another and thus approaching a solution gradually. This procedure seems to be suitable, because the main working functions and their compatibility must be solved first. A morphological matrix, as used in other examples, does not seem to offer any distinct advantages, and may even obscure some of the problems or possible combinations of candidate solutions.

3.1   Establish the inputs and modes of action

3.2   Establish the classes of function-carrier (morphological matrix)

Steps 3.1 and 3.2 are omitted for this case.

3.3   Combine the function-carriers, examine their relationships

The first combination to be attempted, starting from the technological principles shown in Figure 6-4 (1, 2, and 3) and Figure 6-6 (A, B, and C), concerns the functions 'heating' and 'uniting'. These may be realized as sketched in Figure 6-12, where each of the variants of one function-carrier is combined with each variant of the other.

A direct evaluation may now be performed on these combinations, and results in the following assessments:

A-1   Wrong process for tea.

6-12

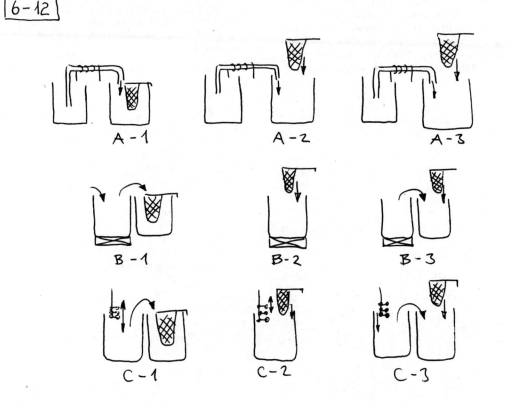

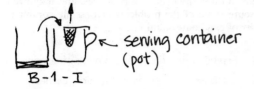

B-1-I ← serving container (pot)

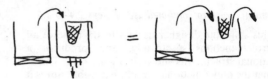

B-1-II

A-2 and **A-3** Water cools before tea leaves are delivered.

B-1 Acceptable.

B-2 Brewing in the heating container is probably unacceptable, due to water hardness depositing on the chamber wall.

B-3 More complicated than B-1, and with similar disadvantage to A-3.

C-1 Unnecessary movement of the heating element.

C-2 As B-2.

C-3 As C-1 and A-3.

This coarse selection results in just one solution as optimal, probably the simplest, and with no obvious disadvantages: B-1.

The designer now chooses to add the technological principle for 'separation', Figure 6-9 (I, II and III). Contrary to the usual preferred procedure (combine the solutions and subsequently evaluate), the designer considers that variant III is unnecessarily complicated, and is in fact a combination of the principles of the other two variants. Principle I is characterized by the fact that the serving container *may* be identical

to the brewing container, whereas principle II implies that they *must* be separate entities; see Figure 6-13.

Solution B-1-I has the advantage of taking up less space; but its major disadvantages are that a mechanical system (for separation) has to interact with a serving/brewing container, and a place has to be found to deliver the spent tea leaves without dripping. The problems to be solved with B-1-I are difficult, and the advantages relatively few. The designer's choice is solution B-1-II.

Review of step 2.3

A consequence of selecting the combination B-1-II is that the two functions 'transport water' and 'transport tea liquid' must be added to the selected technical process (Figure 6-5a). This extension to the functional structure is shown in Figure 6-14.

Technological principles to provide the means for realizing these added functions are shown in Figure 6-15. The following solutions may now be rejected for the reasons stated:

3 How can the siphon tube be filled?

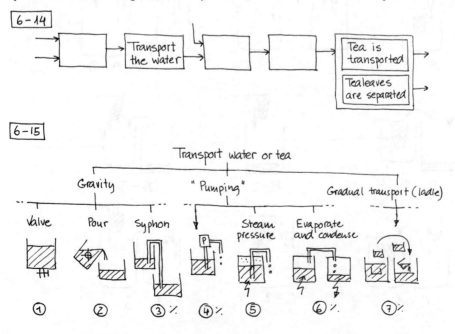

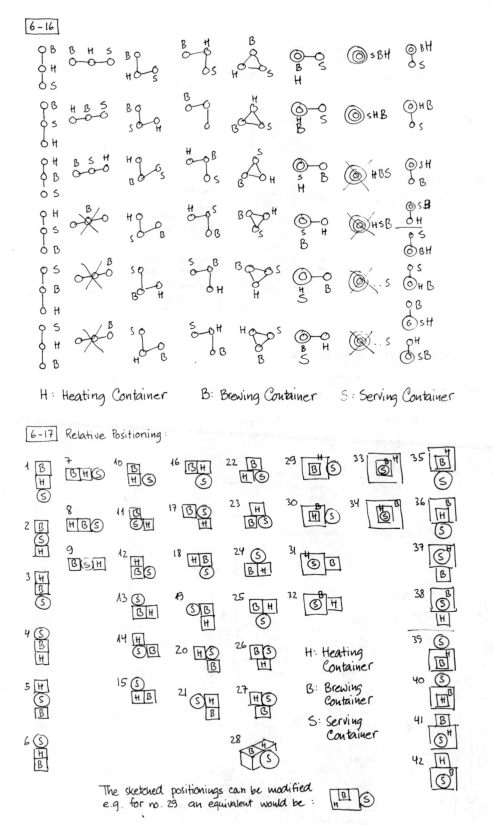

6-16

H: Heating Container   B: Brewing Container   S: Serving Container

6-17 Relative Positioning:

H: Heating Container

B: Brewing Container

S: Serving Container

The sketched positionings can be modified
e.g. for no. 29 an equivalent would be : [H][B] (S)

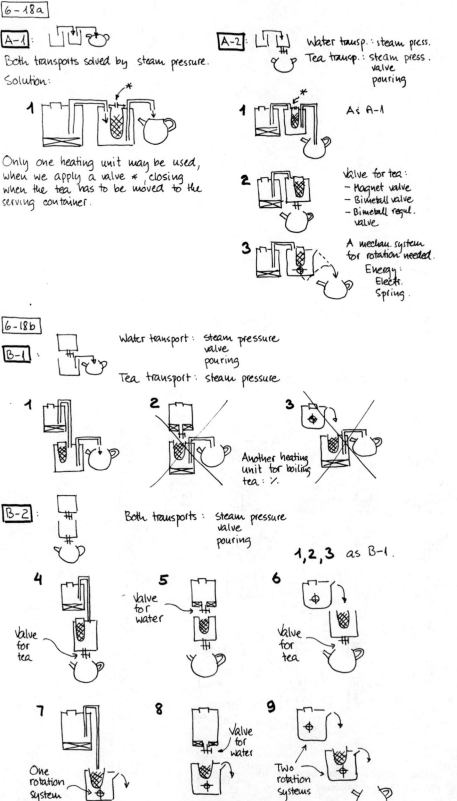

6-18a

A-1: Both transports solved by steam pressure.

Solution:

Only one heating unit may be used, when we apply a valve * closing when the tea has to be moved to the serving container.

A-2: Water transp.: steam press.
Tea transp.: steam press.
valve
pouring

1 As A-1

2 Valve for tea:
– Magnet valve
– Bimetall valve
– Bimetall regul. valve

3 A mechan. system for rotation needed.
Energy:
Electr.
Spring.

6-18b

B-1: Water transport: steam pressure
valve
pouring
Tea transport: steam pressure

1

2 Another heating unit for boiling tea: ✗.

3

B-2: Both transports: steam pressure
valve
pouring

1,2,3 as B-1.

4 Valve for tea

5 Valve for water

6 Valve for tea

7 One rotation system

8 Valve for water

9 Two rotation systems

4 Complex, starting problems.
6, 7 Considered sub-optimal.

The remaining three solutions deserve more careful consideration.

3.4 Establish the basic arrangements

The three main function-carriers of the tea machine decided at this point are: the heating containment (H), the brewing containment (B), and the serving containment (S). A large number of spatial arrangements are possible, especially as these parts each have approximately the same volume. The designer now brainstorms to sketch front views of the possible spatial arrangements. Figure 6-16 shows a rough evaluation which helps to eliminate those that are not feasible. The remaining arrangement proposals are represented in Figure 6-17, using symbols that are easier to visualize. These arrangements are numbered in sequence for reference.

[Note that the designer has now substituted the word 'containment' to imply the function rather than the physical component 'container' that may be designed to carry the function. This move towards a more abstract term can open other possibilities for solving some problems, by freeing the mind of preconceptions.]

The spatial arrangements of the available liquid transport mechanisms 'gravity/valve', 'gravity/top pouring', and 'steam pressure' must also be considered (Figure 6-15). The first two demand that (a) the heating containment is placed above the brewing containment to allow easy transportation of water, and/or (b) the brewing containment is placed above the serving containment to allow easy transport of the liquid tea. Using steam pressure to move the liquids does not impose any restrictions on spatial arrangements.

Further analysis of the proposals in Figure 6-17 reveals that the liquid transport mechanisms can occur in four distinct groups according to the spatial arrangement of the three main elements, A-1, A-2, B-1 and B-2 as shown in Figure 6-18. Considering the transport mechanisms in more detail yields nine distinct candidate solutions based on combining the three transport mechanisms in all possible ways (numbered 1 to 9). Two of these arrangements can be rejected on inspection.

3.5 Σ Concepts
Improve   Evaluate, decide   Verify

The outline concepts developed above raise some basic questions:

● Can a valve to regulate the flow of tea be accepted (cleanliness, taste)?
● Can a valve for water flow be accepted (hardness deposits)?
● Is it feasible to move water or tea by steam pressure (sealing, maximum pressure, safety)?
● How complicated is a mechanical system for pouring?

Working from these questions the designer is able to judge the solutions with regard to such properties as 'functional reliability' and 'simplicity'.

At this stage, solution 1 in Figure 6-18 is selected, using steam pressure to transport the liquid in both stages. However, this solution is not yet complete since the principles for incorporating the 'heating', 'control and regulation' and any necessary auxiliary functions have not yet been specified.

Review of step 3.3
The designer must now add the newly recognized principles and functions. This results in Figure 6-19, which shows the total concept developed from the earlier steps, and containing the following:

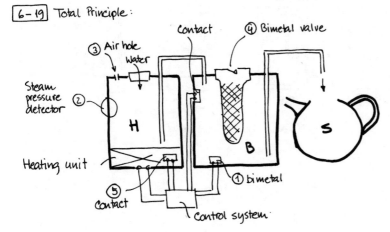

6-19 Total Principle:

6-20

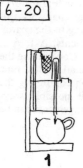

1

Problematic tubing

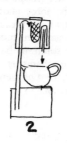

2

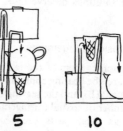

4

∴ Tubing
∴ Appearance

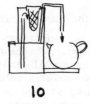

5

Tubing

10

22-1

22-2

∴ Form of
brewing container
22-1 better

23-1

∴ Brewing
container

23-2

∴ Appearance

24-1

24-2

∴ Complicated
∴ appearance

26-1

∴ Brewing
container

26-2

27-1

∴ Tubing

27-2

∴ Brewing
container

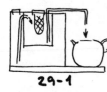

29-1

29-2 Better
(cheaper, easy to
operate)

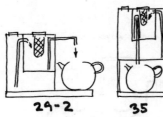

29-2

35

∴ Tubing

39-1

39-2 Better

39-2

- A thermal sensor (1) for regulating the brewing time by sensing the decreasing liquid temperature.
- A steam pressure sensor in the heating vessel (2) for regulating the water heating cycle: heating must be interrupted when the pressure drops after the hot water has been transferred from the heating vessel to the brewing vessel.
- Regulation of the water transport from the heating vessel to the brewing vessel by means of a small bleed hole (3). This ensures that water only starts to move at 100°C, because sufficient pressure only builds up after the steam reaches the critical velocity through this hole (the speed of sound in the fluid passing through the hole).
- A self-acting valve (4), probably working on a bimetal principle, designed to shut after the water transfer is almost completed, and reacting to the increased temperature in the brewing vessel during filling. This valve must be maintained in a closed position by steam pressure during the extraction process.
- A thermal sensor (5) to switch off the heater.

Review of step 3.4

The considerations in Figure 6-17 have helped the designer to identify and choose the means needed for the various operations of moving the liquids. This choice, as developed in Figures 6-18 and 6-19, allows the designer to select almost any of the spatial arrangements of Figure 6-17. The available choices are shown in Figure 6-20. From these results, the designer decides to investigate several solutions, based on an appropriate set of criteria such as:

- Easy operation
- Low price
- Small space requirement
- Reliable operation
- Good appearance

These properties are not easily observable from the sketches in Figure 6-20, and some additional details need to be added to assist the choice between the candidate concepts.

Review of step 3.5

Figure 6-20 also contains a coarse, qualitative evaluation of the arrangements, performed after all the alternatives have been sketched. This shows that seven of the solutions appear to the designer to be better than the rest.

The designer now elaborates each of the remaining solutions, by sketching alternative embodiments of these seven ideas. These are executed mainly as perspective drawings or sketches (which we might think of as three-dimensional graphical models), with some comments. A final evaluation of the concepts uses the criteria in the list above, and the weighting factors and point ratings outlined in Figure 6-2. Examples of this work are shown in Figures 6-21, 6-22 and 6-23.

It is now possible for the designer to perform a more detailed evaluation, the results of which are shown in Figure 6-24. The designer uses a relative costing supported by experience for this assessment of price. A proper evaluation of reliability is difficult at this stage, so this assessment is not included. The result of this evaluation, coupled with intuition and experience, is that solutions 24-1 and 39-2 are selected for further investigation. These two solutions have many features in common and the subsequent work deals with both simultaneously.

Optimal concept

4 Aim: establish the preliminary layouts

4.1 Establish the orientation points for form determination

As the results of design work become more concrete, further design problems emerge. They are concerned particularly with the functional and supporting surfaces, especially those shown in Figure 6-25.

4.2 Establish the arrangements, investigate re-use, rough form-giving, partial dimensioning

Details of form of the important functional surfaces are now investigated. In many cases it is possible to use past experience, to employ standard parts or methods, or to re-use existing items from previous design tasks.

The designer recognizes that the relationships between the top closures and the containers are important. Various types of movable connections between a closure device and the top of a container are proposed and sketched in Figure 6-26. This diagram also shows some of the designer's thoughts on securing the closure against loss and combining it with a rising tube.

Positioning and sealing the rising tubes to the container allows the designer systematically to produce variations of such aspects as support, sealing and fixing. Some of the alternatives are shown in Figure 6-27.

4.3 Establish the types of material, classes of manufacturing method, tolerances and surface properties where necessary

4.4 Investigate the critical form-determination zones

Comments refer to combined use of steps 4.3 and 4.4.

Other aspects of form are also critical for function, cost and the appearance of the proposed tea machine.

6-21   Preliminary layouts ① :

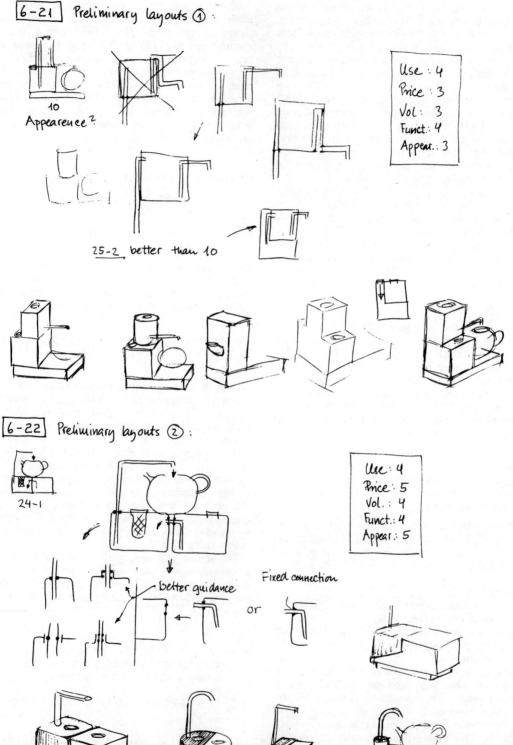

10

Appearence ?

25-2 better than 10

| Use : 4 |
| Price : 3 |
| Vol : 3 |
| Funct : 4 |
| Appear. : 3 |

6-22   Preliminary layouts ② :

24-1

Better guidance

Fixed connection

or

| Use : 4 |
| Price : 5 |
| Vol. : 4 |
| Funct. : 4 |
| Appear. : 5 |

6-23   Preliminary layouts ③ :

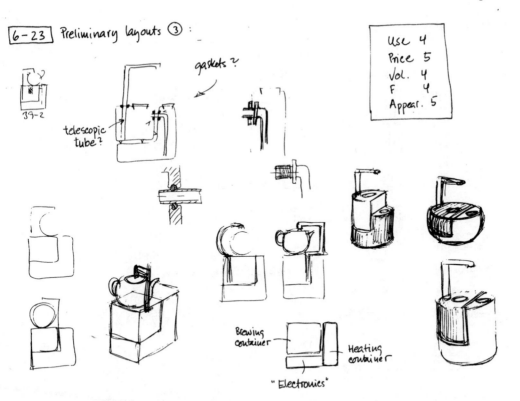

gaskets ?

telescopic tube ?

39-2

Use 4
Price 5
Vol. 4
F 4
Appear. 5

Brewing container

Heating container

"Electronics"

6-24   Evaluation :

Property :	Solution: (see Fig. 6-20) Weight:	2	10 (Fig. 6-21)	22-1	24-1 (Fig. 6-22)	26-2	27-2	39-2 (Fig. 6-23)
Easy to operate	5	5/25	4/20	5/25	4/20	4/20	4/20	4/20
Low price	5	3/15	3/15	3/15	5/25	4/20	3/15	5/25
Small space consumption	3	5/15	3/9	4/12	4/12	3/9	2/6	4/12
Reliable function	4	4/-	4/-	4/-	4/-	4/-	4/-	4/-
Good appearance	4	4/16	3/12	4/16	5/20	4/16	3/12	5/20
	Sum:	71	56	68	77	65	53	77

6-25 Functional surfaces:

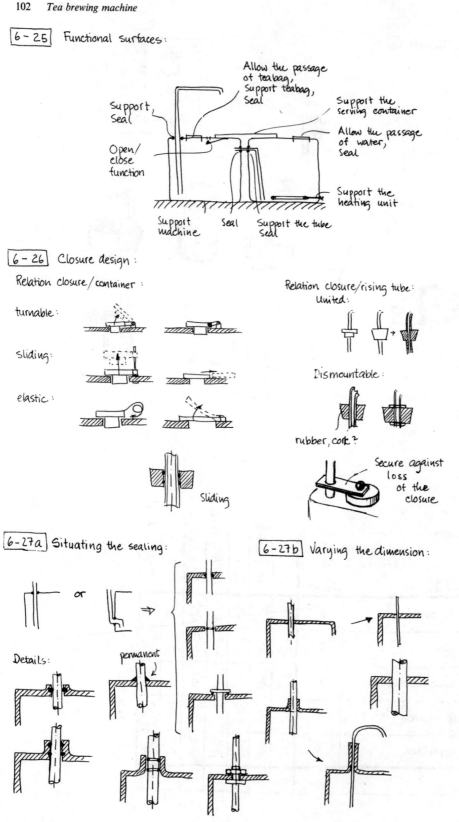

Allow the passage
of teabag,
Support teabag,
Seal

Support,
Seal

Support the
serving container

Allow the passage
of water,
Seal

Open/
close
function

Support the
heating unit

Support
machine

Seal

Support the tube
Seal

6-26 Closure design:

Relation closure/container:

turnable:

sliding:

elastic:

Sliding

Relation closure/rising tube:
United:

Dismountable:

rubber, cork?

Secure against
loss
of the
closure

6-27a Situating the sealing:

or   ⇒

Details:

permanent

6-27b Varying the dimension:

6-28 Support of the tea bag (tea leaf separation):

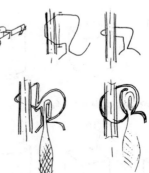

6-29 Control:

Permit space between knob and numbers

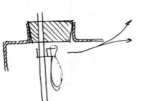

Low height
Large numbers

Larger height, small numbers

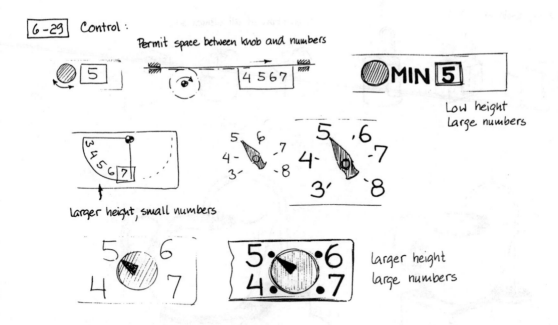

Larger height
large numbers

The following figures show some of the designer's work.

- Figure 6-28: holding a tea-leaf container. The designer has decided that the general 'porous container' used in previous diagrams need not be separately designed, and that a conventional tea bag is the most appropriate holder for tea leaves.
- Figure 6-29: scales and operating knobs.

4.5 Represent the preliminary layouts

- Figure 6-30: integrating the forms for the overall appearance of the device.

4.6 Σ Preliminary layout
Improve Evaluate, decide Verify

- Figure 6-31: two sketches of complete proposals.

6-30a Form integration:

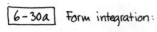

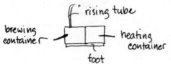

Heating + brewing container:

Heating + brewing container + foot:

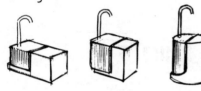

Heating container + foot:

6-30b Form integration:

Brewing
container + foot:

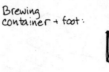

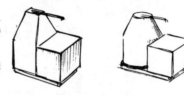

Brewing container + rising tube:

Integration of all elements:

6-31a

6-31b

On presenting the results of this design work to the project sponsor, it is concluded that the resulting tea machine is technically feasible but likely to be too expensive to be successfully marketed. The designer is commended for the thorough and systematic approach that was adopted, but the project is terminated.

Concluding steps 5.1 to 6.7 are redundant for this case.

Case 7   Wave-powered bilge pump

The subject of this case study is a pumping device to remove from a boat water that has accumulated while the boat was unattended. It was undertaken as a design exercise by a group of four first-year students at the Technical University of Denmark.

The conduct of this case shows that the student group is inexperienced. They rely mainly on subjective and intuitive assessments, and seem to be unwilling to follow and critically evaluate the systematic design process that is recommended. As a result some of their work tends to be repetitive, involving the need in some of the later steps to revise and add to the considerations that they glossed over at earlier stages.

Introduction

Those who keep boats in the water for most of the year often suffer problems caused by water ingress to the hull due to rain and leakage. Use of an automatic electric bilge pump to keep this water under control is uneconomical, and use of a hand-operated pump or a hand bailer is time-consuming and requires frequent visits to check the state of the bilges.

The natural movement of a boat on the waves can provide sufficient energy to remove bilge water, if a suitable technical system can be made. The students are given the task of designing a self-acting pump for removing water from a boat's bilges as it accumulates.

Problem assignment

1   Aim: elaborate or clarify the assigned specification

1.1   Critically recognize the assigned problem

1.2   Establish the state of the art

1.3   Analyse the problem situation

Comments refer to combined use of steps 1.1 to 1.3.
The design group's first task is to gather information and generate statements about the needs, to formulate the problems to be solved. For this purpose, the group decides to use brainstorming to formulate a list of questions, conditions and factors concerning the need. These are grouped into categories, each of which should receive deeper and more systematic treatment. A table showing the relationships between various categories and factors is produced, part of which is shown in Figure 7-2. Each of the categories is elaborated by means of data charts, one of which is shown in Figure 7-3. The most important sources of information consists of direct observations at moorings, interviews with users, data obtained from the Institute of Meteorology, and experiments (e.g. on mooring forces).

1.4   Examine the possibilities of realization

The data charts are not only used in the first steps, but are gradually expanded and supplemented by various work sheets, such as revised problem statements, and results of experiments. A sample sheet, Figure 7-4, shows experiments to determine the energy available from a mooring. This experiment is very crude, and the results may be questionable, but at this stage of the project the information they obtain is adequate to give 'order-of-magnitude' figures. The group's conclusion, as presented in their work sheet, seems to indicate some lack of understanding of wave motions and the nature of boat moorings.

1.5   Complete the requirements, classify and quantify, set priorities

The design group do not accept the limitations suggested by their supervisor concerning the sizes of boats to be considered, or the type of energy to be used for pumping. They formulate the problem in a more abstract way: 'A system should be designed that continuously seeks to keep the bilge water in a moored boat at an acceptable minimum level. It should be usable in as many types of boat as possible.'

This system is expressed in diagrammatic form; the formulation adopted by the students is shown in Figure 7-5.

1.6   Work out the full design specification (list of requirements)

Each potential solution is characterized by certain properties and their values. The relative importance of the properties which the design group decided to use to assess the quality of each candidate solution is listed in the need profile shown in Figure 7-6. This profile may be disputed, especially with respect to

Figure 7-1

Steps from General Model according to Figure 0.1	Step	Progress of case	Design documents
1 Aim: elaborate or clarify the assigned specification	1.1 1.2 1.3 1.4 1.5 1.6 1.7	Problem assignment → 7-2, 7-3, 7-4, 7-5, 7-6, 7-7	Factors and Data Experiment System Definition Criteria
2 Aim: establish the functional structures	2.1 2.2 2.3 2.4 2.5 2.6 2.7		
3 Aim: establish the concepts	3.1 3.2 3.3 3.4 3.5	7-8 → 7-9, 7-12, 7-13, 7-14, 7-10, 7-11, 7-15	Function-carriers Combinations Basic Arrangement Concept
4 Aim: establish the preliminary layouts	4.1 4.2 4.3 4.4 4.5 4.6		
5 Aim: establish the dimensional layouts	5.1 5.2 5.3 5.4 5.5 5.6	7-16, 7-17	Layout and Assembly
6 Aim: detailing, elaboration	6.1 6.2 6.3 6.4 6.5 6.6 6.7	7-18, 7-19	Prototype

7-2

Bilge Pump	Categories:	1 Energy	2 Capacity	3 Environment	4 Installation	5 Appearance	6 Behaviour pattern of boat owners	7 Price	8 Risks	9 Maintainance	10 Solutions	11		
No.	Factors:												
1	Rainfall	×											
2	Water from leak	×											
3	Covering of the boat	×				×							
4	Boat materials		×	×									
5	Potential buyers					×	×						
6	Boat types	×											
7	Where are b's moored	×	×										
8	Evaporation	×											
9	Behaviour pattern					×							
10	Boat dimensions	×											
11	Aesthetics				×								
12	Capacity	×											
13	Indication of function									×			
14	Frequency of b. motion	×											
66	Water ingress by sailing	×											
67	Syphon-risk?								×				
68	Solar energy									×			

7-3

Category no.: 4 Installation				Project: Bilge Pump Date: ⁹⁄₁₁		
No.	Factor:	Known data:	Collecting data: Info. need / Coll. data	Source	Cross ref.
	Boat facts				
6	Boat types	Installation depending on boat types, see Encl. B p.5			
24	Boat materials	Wood, Glass fibres reinf. plast. (GRP)			
46	Connecting to boat	Bolts, screws			
30	Leakage	GRP is destroyed, if water leaks between the layers!			
33	Place in boat?	} See Encl. B p5			
47	Available space				
19	Weight of pump		"A pump may weigh up to 5 kg. 10 kg is too much for small craft sailing"	Interview see [10]	
	Facts on owners				
12	Behaviour	Want to install the pump by themselves (do-it-yourself)			
11	Aesthetics				See Cat. 7
50	Boat style				
22	Price	See Category 7			
52	Manual Service				
20	Assembly				

7 - 4   Worksheet sample

No.: 1   of: 6   Date: 12/9   Sign: *lllllla*   Encl.: B   Page: 12

Item: Measuring of mooring forces, Hvidovre Harbour

Experimental conditions: Wind strength: force 6, relative good sea in the harbour, even though this harbour is well protected (between Zeeland and Amager Island).

The experimental equipment consists of a 5l container, a pulley, a string with marks for each 100 mm, and a supporting bar.

Boat: 4m wooden dinghy.

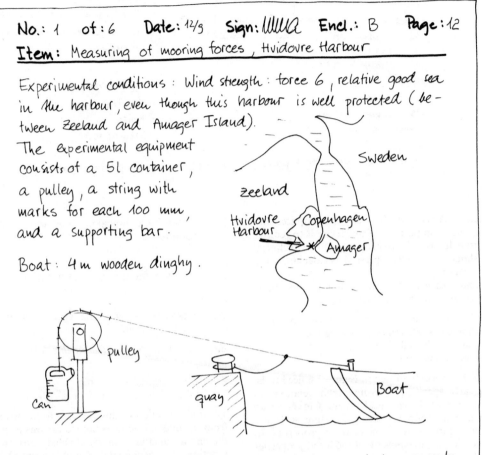

With 5l water in the container, we measured 40 mm short movements every 2 second. Maximum movements every 10 second: 70 mm. Same result with 3l and 1l water.

Energy: $\dfrac{5 \times 9.81 \times 40 \times 10^{-3}}{2}$ $kg \cdot \dfrac{m/s^2 \cdot m}{s}$ $\approx$ 1 watt.

The real energy is bigger due to longer movements and is apparently independent of the container weight.

[* Instructors note: This experiment really does not indicate what energy can be REMOVED from the mooring rope. The falling container puts as much energy back into the boat as the boat delivered to raise the container (minus friction losses).]

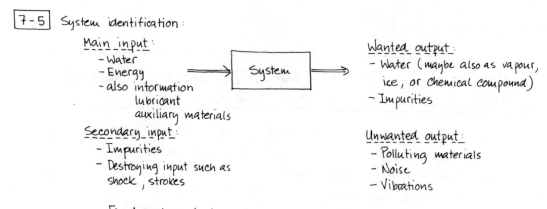

7-5 System identification:

Main input:
- Water
- Energy
- also information
  lubricant
  auxiliary materials

Secondary input:
- Impurities
- Destroying input such as shock, strokes

System

Wanted output:
- Water (maybe also as vapour, ice, or chemical compound)
- Impurities

Unwanted output:
- Polluting materials
- Noise
- Vibrations

Fixed requirement to system: to be used in normal pleasure boats

'sufficient capacity', which is a prime requirement. After all, the main purpose of the device is to remove water from a boat. This property of the technical system should have been expressed as a demand for a stated capacity.

In some respects, the list contains too many properties. It could be simplified to:

● Simple construction (especially in view of price, servicing costs, reliability, and long life)
● Easy use and installation
● Universal application

Some of the properties listed in Figure 7-6 need to be more clearly specified regarding their relationship with the value of the technical system. Curves set up by the design group proposing a rating scale are shown in Figure 7-7 for some of these properties. In principle, the relationships of all the listed properties should be defined by such curves or by comparisons with the qualities of similar equipment.

1.7   Prepare and plan for problem-solving

Design specification

2 Aim: establish the functional structures

2.1   Abstract: produce the black box representations

2.2   Establish the technological principles
       Establish the sequence of operations

2.3   Establish the technical processes,
       TP → optimal TP

2.4   Apply the technical systems and establish boundaries

2.5   Establish the grouping of functions

2.6   Establish the functional structures, and represent them

Steps 2.1 to 2.6 are omitted for this case.

2.7   Σ Functional structures
       Improve   Evaluate, decide   Verify

The main function of this device is to 'remove water' from the bilges. Energy is needed for this purpose, so the main function can be divided into two sub-functions: 'water REMOVE' and 'energy SUPPLY'. This statement represents the functional structure proposed by the group for this problem.

This seems a very crude form for the optimal functional structure, but it may be justified in this problem by the fact that all other functions depend heavily on the conceptual solutions chosen for these two functions.

Optimal functional structure

3 Aim: establish the concepts

3.1   Establish the inputs and modes of action

Step 3.1 is omitted for this case.

3.2   Establish the classes of function-carrier (morphological matrix)

As a first step in their search for solutions, the group uses brainstorming to generate some partial solutions

7-6 Property profile:

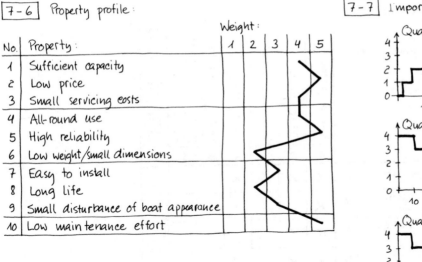

No.	Property:	Weight: 1	2	3	4	5
1	Sufficient capacity					
2	Low price					
3	Small servicing costs					
4	All-round use					
5	High reliability					
6	Low weight/small dimensions					
7	Easy to install					
8	Long life					
9	Small disturbance of boat appearance					
10	Low maintenance effort					

7-7 Important ratings:

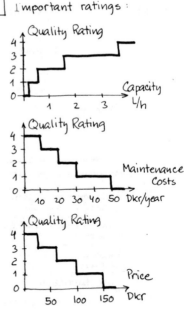

for each of the two major sub-functions, which they enter on the 'morphological axes' in Figure 7-8. They select the most promising or feasible solutions by intuition, and mark them in the matrix. Most of these marked solutions carry some risk, and require deeper investigation.

These conceptual solutions, represented by the crosses in Figure 7-8, cannot be evaluated against the criteria stated above because their magnitudes or properties were inadequately defined. In order to find some properties that can be evaluated at this stage of design, the combined solutions to the two functions are sketched as proposals and investigated on a set of work sheets, some of which are shown in Figure 7-9.

3.3 Combine the function-carriers, examine their relationships

The sketched solutions are then compared, using the criteria of Figure 7-6. Even though most of the properties to be evaluated are not sufficiently well defined in these solutions, a rough choice made by the group reduces the number of solutions for further consideration to six:

1. Pump driven by some appropriate type of windmill
2. Pump driven by a moving mass, energized by boat movements
3. Pump in the boat driven by mooring forces
4. Pump outside the boat driven by mooring forces
5. Pumping using osmosis
6. Electrically driven pump with automatic controller

3.4 Establish the basic arrangements

Evaluating these six proposed solutions needs a clearer understanding and better knowledge of the required properties. The design group again uses a work-sheet approach, in which each solution is explored by sketches, calculations and experiments, and the results are collected on hand-written sheets. The example of these sheets shown in Figure 7-10 concerns the two proposals for pumps inside and outside the boat driven by motion relative to the mooring.

3.5 Σ Concepts
Improve Evaluate, decide Verify

The design group performs a detailed evaluation of the eight proposals. They use a weighted rating, and establish the weightings on the basis of the need profile shown in Figure 7-6. The rating chart is shown in Figure 7-11.

The properties suggested as criteria either need very detailed investigation or some of the criteria must be ignored before a reasonable evaluation can be made. Only those few criteria covered by the above investigations are used in this evaluation.

In this case study the group has made subjective evaluations and judgements, and allowed themselves to make decisions unsupported by the data and information that they list in their proposals. Pressure of time also forces a choice. The group decides to continue only with solution 5, even though solution 2 is assessed as having about equal merit and quality.

7-8 Morphological scheme:

"Energy source": \ "Remove water":		Positive displacement pump	Other pumps	Mechanical carrier	Evaporator	System decomposing the water	Systems based on osmosis	System utilizing variations in water level
		1	2	3	4	5	6	7
Movements in the air	A	×	×		×			
Boat movement relative to quay or mooring post	B	×						×
Boat movement relative to water	C	×	×					
Electrical accumulater	D	×	×		×	×		
Fuels, Lubricants	E	×	×					
The sun (solar energy)	F				×			
Temperature differences	G	×						
Temperature variations	H	×						
Differences in concentration	i			×	×		×	
Reactive compounds	J				×	×		
Falling rain	K	×						
Wave movements	L	×						×
Pressure variations	M							
Water movement relative to quay or mooring post	N	×						×

After deciding on the working principle for the pump the group chooses a more systematic approach for establishing the optimal concept: they establish the functions required for the pump, search for solutions, and combine these solutions into a concept.

Review of step 2.7
The student group identifies the following functions for the pump:

1. Form a space of varying volume
2. Provide a non-return function to prevent reverse flow
3. Return the pump to its initial state after activation by the mooring line
4. Permit connection of the pump to the mooring rope
5. Permit assembly of the intake and/or outlet tubes to the pump

Review of steps 3.3 and 3.4
In the following steps, the solution principles for these functions are established by employing logical considerations.

1. The space of varying volume may be realized by
   (a) relative movement of rigid bodies, e.g. a piston in a cylinder
   (b) changes of form in flexible bodies
   (c) combinations of these
2. The valve function may be actuated by sensing
   (a) the pressures
   (b) the tension forces in the pump
   (c) the relative movements in the pump parts
   (d) the extreme positions of the moving parts

These two primary functions are shown in Figure 7-12. The sketch layouts (concepts) in Figure 7-13 are developed from these principles.

3. The nature of a rope mooring will only allow transmission of tension, so any mechanism must have a means of returning it to its initial position after actuation. This implies that some energy must be stored in a spring or a mass raised under gravity.

7–9 Worksheet

Item: Solutions

A–1: Air stream + positive displacement pump.

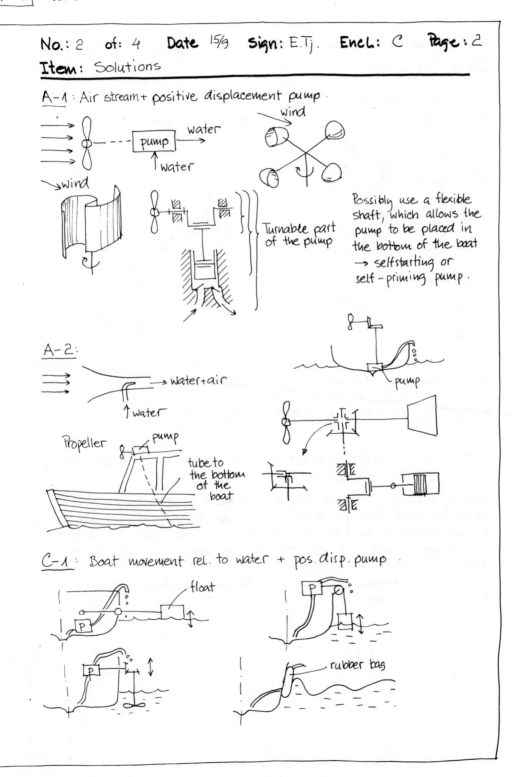

water

pump

↑water

wind

wind

Turnable part of the pump

Possibly use a flexible shaft, which allows the pump to be placed in the bottom of the boat → selfstarting or self-priming pump.

A–2:

→ water+air

↑water

pump

Propeller   pump

tube to the bottom of the boat

C–1: Boat movement rel. to water + pos. disp. pump.

float

P

P

P

rubber bag

7-9   Worksheets cont.:

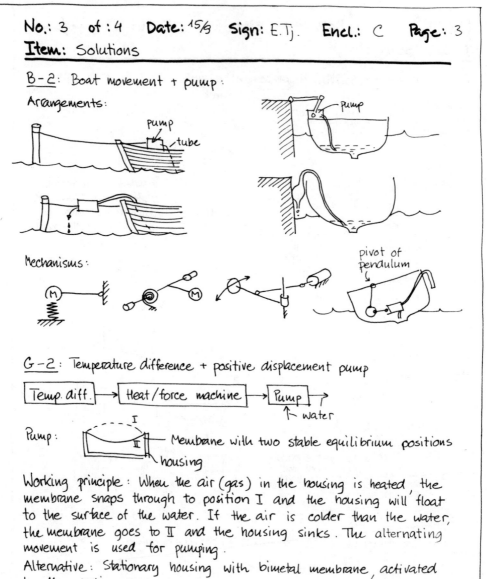

No.: 3   of : 4   Date: 15/6   Sign: E.Tj.   Encl.: C   Page: 3
Item: Solutions

B-2: Boat movement + pump:
Arrangements:

Mechanisms:

pivot of pendulum

G-2: Temperature difference + positive displacement pump

| Temp. diff. | → | Heat/force machine | → | Pump | → |

↑ water

Pump: I   II   — Membrane with two stable equilibrium positions

housing

Working principle: When the air (gas) in the housing is heated, the membrane snaps through to position I and the housing will float to the surface of the water. If the air is colder than the water, the membrane goes to II and the housing sinks. The alternating movement is used for pumping.

Alternative: Stationary housing with bimetal membrane, activated by the washing seas.

7-9 Worksheets cont. :

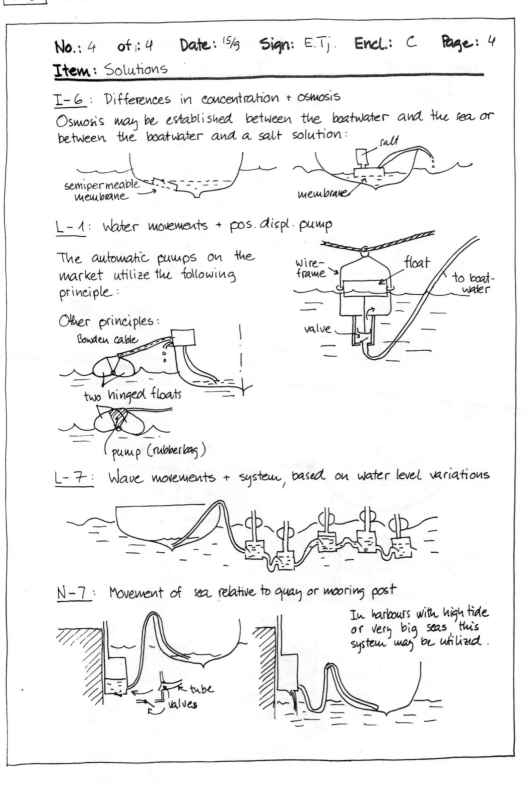

No.: 4   of: 4   Date: 15/9   Sign: E.Tj.   Encl.: C   Page: 4

Item: Solutions

I-6 : Differences in concentration + osmosis

Osmosis may be established between the boatwater and the sea or between the boatwater and a salt solution:

salt

semipermeable membrane

membrane

L-1: Water movements + pos. displ. pump

The automatic pumps on the market utilize the following principle:

wire-frame   float   to boat-water

valve

Other principles:

Bowden cable

two hinged floats

pump (rubberbag)

L-7: Wave movements + system, based on water level variations

N-7: Movement of sea relative to quay or mooring post

In harbours with high tide or very big seas this system may be utilized.

tube
valves

7-10 Worksheet

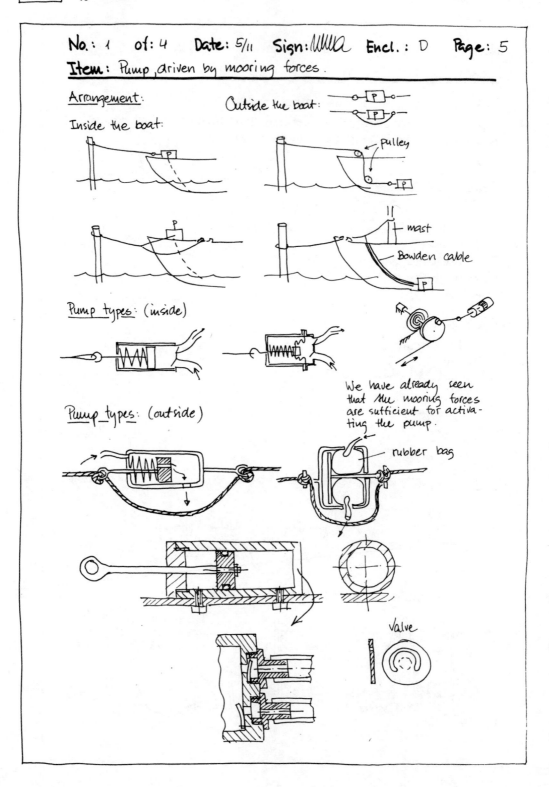

No.: 1 of: 4 Date: 5/11 Sign: MMMa Encl.: D Page: 5

Item: Pump, driven by mooring forces.

Arrangement:

Outside the boat:

Inside the boat:

Pulley

mast

Bowden cable

Pump types: (inside)

Pump types: (outside)

We have already seen that the mooring forces are sufficient for activating the pump.

rubber bag

Valve

7-11 Evaluation

Solutions:	No	Sufficient capacity	Low price	Small servicing costs	All-round use	High reliability	Low weight Small	Easy to install	Long life	Small disturbance of boat appearance	Low maintenance effort	Σ_{max} 144	$\frac{\Sigma}{144}$
Properties:		1	2	3	4	5	6	7	8	9	10	Σ	$\frac{\Sigma}{144}$
Weight*		4	5	4	4	5	2	3	2	3	5		
1. Propeller with pump placed by the propeller		4	2	4	4	3	3	3	2	2	3	113	0.79
2. Positive disp. pump driven by moving mass		4	2	4	3	3	3	4	3	4	4	118	0.87
3. Positive disp. pump driven by a cable connected to the mooring		4	2	4	3	3	3	3	2	3	3	112	0.78
4. Positive disp. pump driven direct by the mooring, placed in boat		4	2	4	2	3	3	3	2	2	3	105	0.73
5. Same, placed outside boat		4	4	4	3	3	4	4	2	3	3	127	0.88
6. Osmosis between boat water and a saltwater reservoir		2	3	1	3	3	1	4	4	4	2	98	0.68
7. Osmosis between boat water and the sea		1	3	3	1	2	3	3	4	3	2	87	0.60
8. Electrically driven pump with automatic control		4	2	2	4	3	4	3	2	4	3	113	0.79

* See Fig. 7-6

7-12 Changing volumes: Valves:

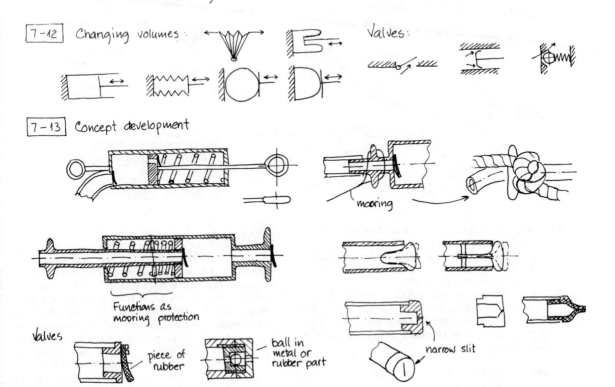

7-13 Concept development

mooring

Functions as mooring protection

Valves

piece of rubber

ball in metal or rubber part

narrow slit

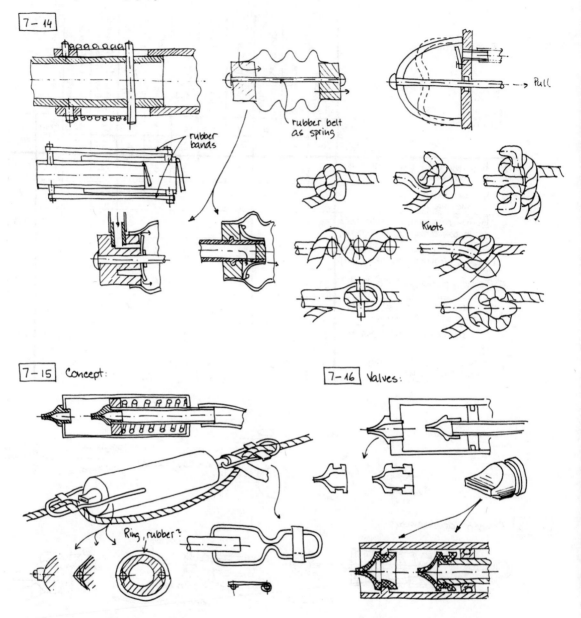

7-14

7-15 Concept:

7-16 Valves:

rubber bands

rubber belt as spring

Pull

Knots

Ring, rubber?

4. There are at least two possibilities for accommodating the mooring force:
   (a) the pump is required to transmit the full force
   (b) the mooring rope takes over when the force exceeds a specified limit
5. The intake tube for this outboard pump will only experience external pressure (suction from the bilge region to the pump). The connections to the pump can therefore be simple, providing that it is self-sealing.

These considerations lead to the solution proposals shown in Figure 7-14.

Review of step 3.5

Various combinations of these solutions are seen to be possible, and they lead to a set of concepts. A systematic approach would consist of presenting a number of such concepts in sketch form, and trying to evaluate them by using the criteria shown in Figure 7-6, possibly in a more detailed form. The students are now advised that they should verify the properties of their proposed pumping arrangement by making an appropriate functional model of the pump in hardware. Pressure of time forces them to make an intuitive choice of one concept for further work, the concept shown in Figure 7-15.

Optimal concept

4 Aim: establish the preliminary layouts

4.1 Establish the orientation points for form determination

4.2 Establish the arrangements, investigate re-use, rough form-giving, partial dimensioning

Comments refer to combined use of steps 4.1 and 4.2.

The group's main activity in these steps is to establish some major dimensions for the pump, and to select materials and the basic form of all elements. The aim is to obtain an anatomical structure of the pump and its support, thus supplying the basis for form determination and detail.

Initially the piston diameter and stroke can be established by calculation, using limiting conditions such as:

- Force available is less than 10 N
- Suction should produce a pressure drop of about 20 kPa

Calculations show that a force of 5 N is enough to take up the slack the mooring rope. Two possibilities present themselves: (a) to let the spring push the water out of the pump, or (b) to let the spring suck the water into the pump.

The spring for alternative (b) would need to be stronger than that required for (a), because the water being expelled from the pump only needs to overcome the pressure drop caused by the valve. Alternative (a) would have a further advantage of being more likely to be self-priming, because any pull on the mooring rope will move the pump. Alternative (b) is likely to prime only if the duration and force of the mooring pull are sufficient, as might be expected in heavier wave motion. The force-displacement relationship could be made strongly progressive, thereby forming a type of shock absorber that could provide mooring protection.

The earlier experiments apparently show that the relationship of mooring force over time is such that pulls are shorter than the slack periods between pulls. It thus seems logical to use principle (b), i.e. to use the pulls to expel water from the pump, and to let the spring suck the water from the bilges in the longer idle periods.

(*Comment* This principle seems to be the opposite of that sketched in the concepts developed earlier. Later in this project, the group details a pump following principle (a), and thus neglects these considerations. This is perhaps due to other considerations entering the problem, or to a lack of understanding of the previous work. The students' sketches of

pumps almost invariably show principle (a); they may not be fully aware of additional considerations such as the need either to provide frames around the pump body to transform mooring rope pull into pump body contraction, or to make the smaller space surrounding the piston rod and spring into the working chamber with the need to vent the larger space to atmosphere.)

4.3 Establish the types of material, classes of manufacturing methods, tolerances and surface properties where necessary

4.4 Investigate the critical form-determination zones

Comments refer to combined use of steps 4.3 and 4.4.

The rubber valve is recognized as a crucial element of this pump. It is intended to be used as both suction and pressure valve. The housing is to be made from a nylon compound, with a steel frame inlaid into the body. This frame forms the connection to the mooring rope.

4.5 Represent the preliminary layouts

4.6 Σ Preliminary layout
Improve   Evaluate, decide   Verify

Optimum preliminary layout

5 Aim: establish the dimensional layouts

5.1 Deliver the substantiation for certain design characteristics

5.2 Establish the definitive arrangement, form determination, partial dimensioning

5.3 Establish the definitive and complete determination of materials, manufacturing methods, partial definitive determination of tolerances and surface properties

5.4 Optimize the critical form determination zones

5.5 Represent the dimensional layout

Comments refer to combined use of steps 4.5 to 5.5.

The delivery volume required of this pump is established by considering the lowest frequency

7-17

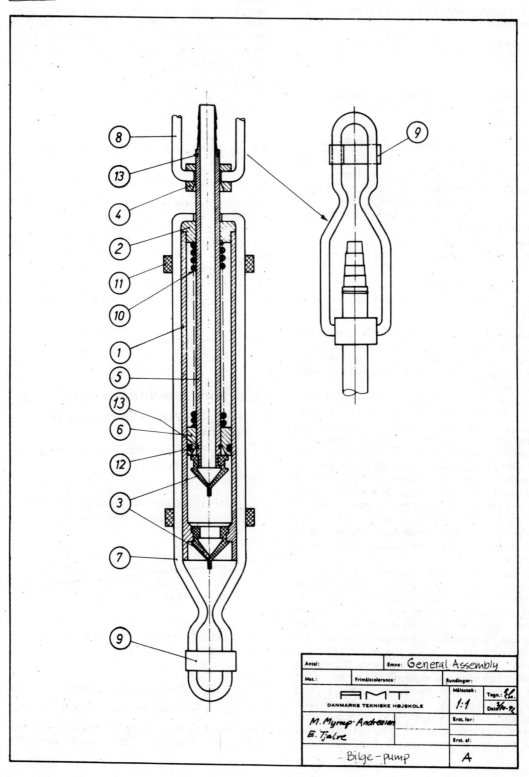

component of the wave motion in the harbour. The pressure drop in the suction tube is calculated to ensure that the energy consumption is low compared to the energy available from the mooring motions. The spring is selected using standard calculation procedures. Most of the remaining dimensions are based on estimation and yield the proportions shown in Figure 7-16. A set of workshop drawings are prepared to enable a prototype to be manufactured. The assembly drawing is shown in Figure 7-17.

5.6 Σ Dimensional layout
 Improve Evaluate, decide Verify

Optimal dimensional layout

Release for detailing

6 Aim: produce details, elaborate

6.1 Deliver the substantiation for detail decisions

Starting from the drawings, two model pumps are produced to test various aspects of this solution. One is a cheap mock-up (Figure 7-18), i.e. a dummy with no interior mechanisms to allow experiments on attaching the proposed pump to the mooring. This is used to study spatial considerations and aesthetic properties.

The second is a functioning prototype model (Figure 7-19). It is based on the mock-up and uses the results of the mounting tests, but is obviously more costly. The appearance of both models is very similar, but the functional model contains materials and parts that are likely to be used in the manufactured product, and is produced to the tolerances and surface finishes thought to be needed for the final items. The valves are moulded from silicone rubber.

The results of experiments performed on this prototype pump may be summarised as follows:

- The valves work adequately.
- The pump capacity is sufficient.
- Positioning and connecting the pump to the mooring rope is satisfactory.
- The suction tube is found to be too big, and the self-priming capability of the pump is not adequate. The self-priming capability could be enhanced by adding a third non-return valve, a footvalve, at the suction end of this tube.

The task set for the student group finishes here. An excerpt from the students' report reads:

'The pump we have designed seems to cover a boat owner's need for a system that clears a boat of any incoming water in a continuous and automatic operation. The pump is easy to mount on a mooring line, and does not detract from the appearance of the boat. Visual checking that the pump is operating is possible from the shore.

'The functional model is made from available materials. Based on the results obtained from our

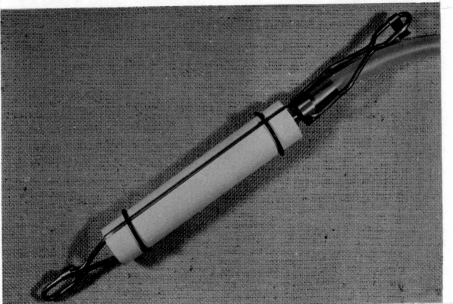

Figure 7-18
Form model

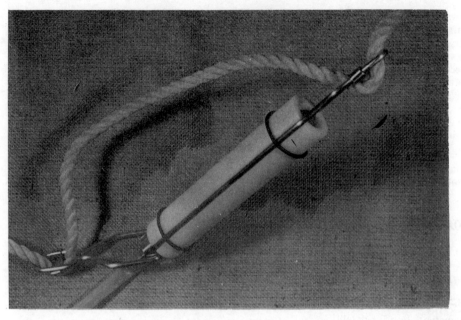

Figure 7-19
Functional model

experiments, we predict a probable production cost of 50 DKr, assuming series production with suitable processes.

'This project still needs much work to produce a saleable commercial product. Only the technical aspects have been treated, but the results provide a good basis for a market investigation.'

Concluding steps 6.2 to 6.7 are not developed for this case.

Case 8 Oil drain valve

This application of a methodical design procedure is unusual in this book because a first layout already exists, and some of the steps in the general procedural model can be omitted as a consequence. In particular, those design characteristics that are concerned with the technical process have already been established, and it would not be rewarding to search for further solutions. This situation is typical of design improvement work in industry, when a portion of the technical system is to remain in its existing form. Applying systematic methods to such a task is considered novel.

Introduction

The overall task is to develop, for a research institute, an existing piece of experimental apparatus to aid the study of sliding bearings. The concept is currently assessed to be very good, but some of the proposed parts are considered to be too expensive. This is particularly true of the means of providing the oil drain and overflow functions for the weighing container used to measure flow-rate. The problem of redesigning this area for lower cost is assigned to the design group. The designers are given the problem statement shown in Figure 8-2, and a layout of the drain valve assembly as proposed by the research department (Figure 8-3).

Problem assignment

1 Aim: elaborate or clarify the assigned specification

1.1 Critically recognize the assigned problem

1.2 Establish the state of the art

1.3 Analyse the problem situation

1.4 Examine the possibilities of realization

1.5 Complete the requirements, classify and quantify, set priorities

1.6 Work out the full design specification (list of requirements)

Comments refer to combined use of steps 1.1 to 1.6.

Even though a first layout exists, it is considered useful for the designer to set up a revised list of requirements in the usual formal fashion, to help with an appropriate selection of evaluation criteria. The

resulting design specification and the geometry of the available space are shown in Figures 8-4 and 8-5.

1.7 Prepare and plan for problem-solving

As this is a special case in which some of the steps in the procedural model can be omitted, the design team plans not to investigate the technical process but to derive the functional structure directly from the given layout (Figure 8-3). The main emphasis is given to the phases of conceptualizing and layout, and studying them in an effort to reduce manufacturing costs.

Design specification

2 Aim: Establish the functional structures

2.1 Abstract: produce the black box representations

2.2 Establish the technological principles
Establish the sequence of operations

2.3 Establish the technical processes,
TP → optimal TP

2.4 Apply technical systems to the process, and establish boundaries

2.5 Establish the grouping of functions

Steps 2.1 to 2.5 were omitted for this case.

The above steps are considered redundant, because the project starts from a problem assignment containing a proposed layout. The functional structure is derived directly from the initial documents, Figures 8-2 and 8-3, and using the information developed for Figures 8-4 and 8-5.

2.6 Establish the functional structures, and represent them

This work proceeds from some established characteristics of the technical process of draining the measuring container:

- Technology, and technological principle – emptying through an opening in the base of the container (which implies that such alternatives as a tilting container or siphoning are not to be considered).

123

Figure 8-1

Steps from General Model according to Figure 0.1	Step	Progress of case	Design documents
1 Aim: elaborate or clarify the assigned specification	1.1 1.2 1.3 1.4 1.5 1.6 1.7	Problem Assignment 8-2, 8-3 8-4 8-5	Design Specification Space Diagram
2 Aim: establish the functional structures	2.1 2.2 2.3 2.4 2.5 2.6 2.7	8-6 8-7	Functional Structure
3 Aim: establish the concepts	3.1 3.2 3.3 3.4 3.5	8-8 8-9 8-10 8-11 8-12 8-13 8-14 8-15	Morphological Matrix Relationship Matrix & Organ Structure Concepts Evaluation
4 Aim: establish the preliminary layouts	4.1 4.2 4.3 4.4 4.5 4.6		
5 Aim: establish the dimensional layouts	5.1 5.2 5.3 5.4 5.5 5.6	8-16 8-17 8-18	Dimensional Layouts Evaluation
6 Aim: detailing, elaboration	6.1 6.2 6.3 6.4 6.5 6.6 6.7		

Figure 8.2   Problem statement

An oil drain organ is to be designed to work with a bearing test apparatus. It should be supplied as a sub-assembly for an existing quantity-measuring device, a flow-rate weighing container. This drain organ, in its closed position, should *completely seal* the container's drain opening, so that the incoming oil quantity can be determined by weighing after a given time. It must then permit *total draining* of the contents. Drainage is to take place by gravity, in the form of a free-falling liquid stream entering without wall contact into an existing round hole in the drain tube. To avoid over-filling the container, the drain organ should also act as an *overflow*, so that after reaching the maximum permitted level all the entering oil is continuously discharged into the drain tube.

The drain sub-assembly is to be fastened to the container: diameter of opening 125 mm, wall thickness of container 3 mm.

Conditions
● Operation should take place by hand.
● Position of the organ (whether open or closed) should be visible from outside the container.
● Both end positions of the organ must be self-retained, by friction or any other means.

● Application and boundaries of the technical system 'oil drain valve' – the valve must ensure both the planned operation of 'draining oil', and the occasional safety operation of 'permitting overflow'.

The variety of solutions is clearly limited.

A useful abstract statement from which the functional structure can be derived is: 'closing an outlet by one fixed and one movable part, with the added effects of reducing the free area and sealing'. The functional structure developed by the design team is shown in Figure 8-6 as a block schematic, and in Figure 8-7 as a function tree.

[The two types of representation of the functional structure allow a comparison of their properties, particularly regarding their content and the availability of information about individual functions and their relationships.]

From the block schematic of the functional structure (Figure 8-6) it is clear that the receptors and effectors in the technical system must interface with the environment:

(a) providing a connection to the fixed parts of the container,
(b) opening or closing the connections to the drain tube (including the overflow arrangement),
(c) forming the action location where the human operator enters information (manual commands) and energy, which move the function-carrier for closure and provide the sealing forces,
(d) issuing information to an observer about the state of the drain opening, whether it is open, partly open, or closed.

[The classification that the designers use to place the individual functions in the function tree (Figure 8-7) is interesting. In particular the questions arise:

(1) When and at what level should these auxiliary, propulsion and control functions that support the main functions be incorporated into the scheme?
(2) Should any of them be shown at more than one position on this function tree, to indicate interactions and relationships that are explicitly shown in the block schematic?

These diagrams show no alternatives to the functions or their sequence. They are derived from the existing layout and problem statement, and are accepted in this form. In the following stages, the design team look for alternative solutions to the more concrete problems.]

2.7   Σ Functional structures
      Improve   Evaluate, decide   Verify

Optimal functional structure

3   Aim: establish the concepts

3.1   Establish the inputs and modes of action

The only inputs to the oil drain valve are manual control, and force and motion to operate it.

The mode of action of the oil drain valve can be described without reference to specific hardware as follows:

● The movement and force provided by the hand is transmitted by the 'activation' function-carrier to the 'closure' function-carrier.
● The movable parts are brought into a new state and position.
● The action motion of the closure parts can be adjusted to produce various flow quantities and rates, and this is accomplished by a particular function-carrier in the technical system.

3.2   Establish the classes of function-carrier (morphological matrix)

In this step, the aim is to find various classes of function-carrier by considering suitable action principles. The functions (or partial functions) are

8-3

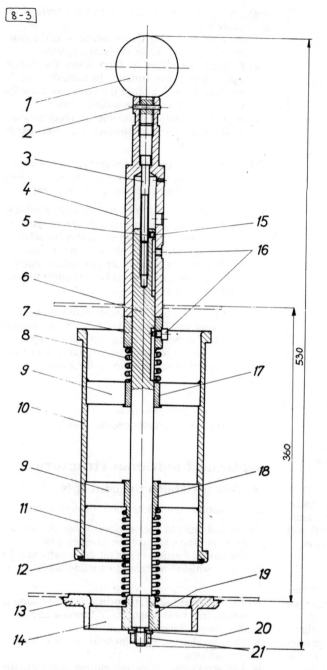

1   Ball Handle, 56 Dia
2   Pin, 3 Dia (m6) × 24 lg
3   Hex Socket Screw (mod.)
4   Sleeve   35 Dia × 190 lg
5   Clamping Disk 3 Dia × 2 thk
6   Rod 23 Dia × 363 lg
7   Spring Guide 35 Dia × 30 lg
8   Spring 32 o/Dia × 30 lg × 4 W/Dia, 5 coil
9   Spoke   20 × 6 × 36 lg
10 Valve Tube 125 o/Dia × 12,5 thk × 204 lg
11 Spring 33 o/Dia × 120 lg × 3W/Dia, 13 coil
12 O-Ring   116/110 Dia × 3
13 Weld Ring
14 Spoke   20 × 6 × 31 lg
15 Grub Screw M4 × 4 lg
16 Hex Socket Screw (mod.)
17 Guide Bush   35 Dia × 25 lg
18 Guide Bush   35 Dia × 32 lg
19 Rod Clamp Bush 35 Dia × 33 lg
20 Plain Washer 10,5/20 × 2 thk
21 Hex Nut   M 10

taken from the functional structure and listed in the first column of a morphological matrix. The candidate solutions for each of the functions are noted in the usual way (Figure 8-8).

[It is interesting that this matrix contains mainly word pictures of the proposed function-carriers, compared to the morphological charts shown in other cases in this book where sketches are used extensively. The more abstract formulation of descriptions in words tends to encourage a more creative interpretation in the problem-solving process. Diagrams and sketches provide clearer reminders, and are easier to understand, but tend to be restrictive since they present preconceived ideas.]

The function-carriers of this technical system also need some auxiliary functions to enable them to be

Figure 8.4 Clarified design specification	*Fixed req.*	*Desire*
1 *Function*		
(1) Drain opening tightly sealed	•	
(2) Permit total emptying	•	
(3) Ensure overflow	•	
2 *Functionally determined properties*		
A Operand		
(1) Lubricating oil	•	
Dynamic viscosity; $0.002–0.1 \, \text{kg m}^{-1}\text{s}^{-1}$		
Density: $880 \, \text{kg m}^{-3}$		
Temperature, normal: 20 to 50°C		
short-term: to 90°C		
(2) Oil flow rate: $1.5 \, \text{kg s}^{-1}$ max.	•	
B Connected systems	•	
(1) Oil container with hole and lid (Figure 8-5)	•	
(2) Free fall into drain tube (Figure 8-5)	•	
(3) No spillage sideways at the hole in the drain tube (no connecting tube from container to drain tube; organ to be adjustable to a limited and quantitatively unknown capability of the drain tube)	•	
(4) Geometric arrangement (Figure 8-5)	•	
(5) Oil container free to move in vertical direction for weighing (about 2 mm)		
(6) No additional forces on container from drain	•	
(7) Lid must be freely removable, with no attachments	•	
C Manipulation, operator	•	
(1) By hand, within the region shown in Figure 8.5		•
(2) Position of drain organ visible when closed or open		•
(3) End positions self-holding		•
(4) Rapid emptying (but consider B2 and B3)		
3 *Operational properties*		•
(1) Life at least 10 years	•	
(2) High reliability		•
(3) Minimum maintenance	•	
(4) Easy checking		
4 *Ergonomic properties*	•	
(1) Ergonomic conditions: hand operation (magnitude of necessary force)		•
(2) Operation by right- or left-handed persons	•	
(3) Clean for operator		
5 *Appearance*		
No requirements (almost nothing visible)		
6 *Manufacturing properties*		
(1) One-off manufacture	•	
(2) Manufacturable in the research institute workshops	•	
7 *Delivery and planning properties*		
Delivery deadline *x* weeks (consider delivery times for bought-out parts)	•	
8 *Manufacturing expenditure*		
Limited financial means, therefore low cost and minimum bought-out items	•	

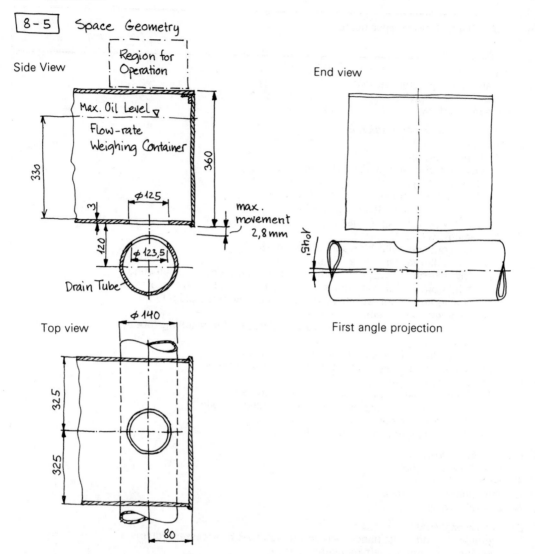

8-5 Space Geometry

Side View

Region for Operation

Max. Oil Level ▽

Flow-rate Weighing Container

330

360

φ125

3

max. movement 2,8mm

120

φ123,5

Drain Tube

End view

Shol

First angle projection

Top view

φ140

325

325

80

effective. A few of these have not yet been entered into the functional structure, e.g. the partial function 'GUIDE' for the movable parts in function 5.

3.3 Combine the function-carriers, examine their relationships

Any attempt to combine function-carriers must consider their compatibility. It is particularly so in this case study, where some of the classes of function-carriers predetermine the nature of some other function-carriers. For instance, if in function 1 a plate- or ball-valve is selected, then the action motion for that function-carrier can only be in a straight line. The choice of corresponding function-carriers for functions 2, 4, and 5 is then restricted.

To aid the selection of compatible arrangements, two forms of design document are found useful (Figure 8-9):

(a) a matrix of relationships between partial functions, where each function-carrier identified in the first column of Figure 8-8 is checked to see whether it has a relationship to another function-carrier (each relationship is checked in turn, but the interactions may not be mutual: one function-carrier may affect but not be affected by another);

(b) an abstract function-carrier structure, in which the relationships are shown as connecting lines between blocks.

It is then possible to establish the concepts as organ structures (structures of function-carriers).

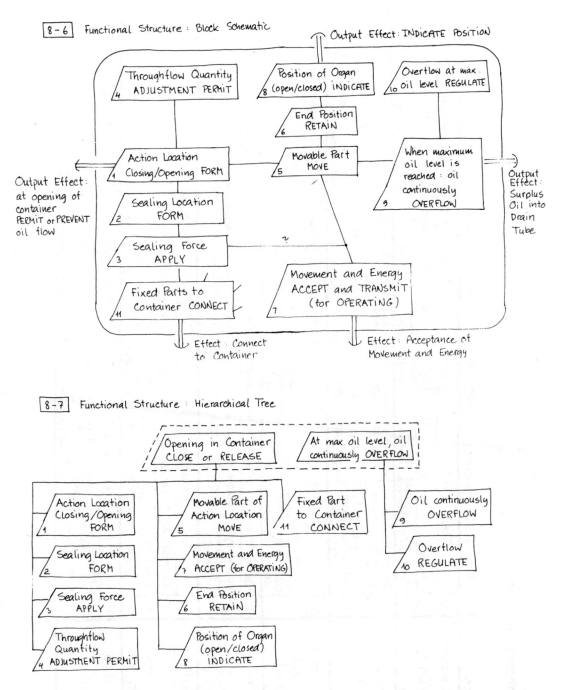

8-6 Functional Structure: Block Schematic

8-7 Functional Structure: Hierarchical Tree

3.4 Establish the basic arrangements

The concept sketches produced by the design team are shown in Figures 8-10 to 8-14, in a form that is as abstract and schematic as possible.

[It is typical, especially for some of the simplest solutions, that such abstract representations are not adequate, because the form of the components contributes substantially to their effects. It is necessary to work with more solid forms which indicate, but do not define, the proportions and dimensions, as shown for Variant 3 (Figure 8-12). Some detail can be shown, but care must be taken that the abstract and general nature of the solution is not destroyed. A fine balance

8-8 Morphological Matrix:

AP .. Action Principle   FC .. Function-Carrier (Organ)

No. 1 — Action Location / Closing/Opening FORM

AP: Cover opening | Close with Peg | Axial control slider in opening

FC:
- Cover opening — Valve (Plate, Ball); Slider (linear motion, rotary motion); Flap
- Close with Peg — cylind. round peg; conical round peg; milled-face cylindrical peg
- Axial control slider in opening — closed cylindrical shell with side openings

No. 2 — Sealing Location FORM

AP: Rigid seal face with elastic counter | Elastic seal element with rigid counter | Plastically deformable seal face | Elastic macrogeometric closure element | Ground-in surfaces

FC:
- Ring on plate or flap / Counter: flat gasket elastic plate
- "O"-ring gasket; flat gasket seal
- lip seal; sharp edge seal
- soft metal seal; elastic valve plate (plastic material)
- elastic ball surface (plastic material); flat surface; cylinder (cone) surface

No. 3 — Sealing Force APPLY and MAINTAIN

AP: Mechanical | Hydraulic | Hydr/Pneu | (Electro-) Magnetic

FC:
- Spring — helical spring (torsion); leaf or rod spring; bulk plastic body
- mass with weight action
- Lip seal with compressing action
- force piston
- Switchable Permanent Magnet; Coil with soft-iron core

No. 4 — Throughflow Quantity ADJUSTMENT PERMIT

AP: Outlet Hole change / Valve opening constant | Outlet Hole const. / Valve Opening change | Change both

FC:
- Interchangeable Diameter Throat; Movable Hole Pattern Plate; Movable Adjustment Plate
- Control with x Defined Positions
- Change geometry of closure Organ; Combine

No. 5 — Movable Part of Action Location MOVE and GUIDE

AP: 1 degree of freedom (Ω rotating, ⟲ Swinging, ↔ sliding) | 2 degrees of freedom (rotation & sliding)

FC:
- rotation sleeve + guide
- flap + guide
- valve gate + guide; gate valve linear motion
- gate + guide

No. 6 — End Position RETAIN

AP: Form Closure | Force Closure

FC:
- Form Closure — Bayonet Connect.; Ratchet; Cross Pin (cotter); Sliding element with Slot-in Feature (Spreader Spring, Ball w. Spring); Toggle Lever over-centre
- Force Closure — Mechanical: Weight (direct weight action, weighted lever system), force applied (clamp Faces, Wedge, Exc., Possible combinations); Magnetic (Switch. Perm. Magnet, Solenoid Coil)

		Mechanical				Pneumatic/Hydraulic	Electro-magnetic
7	Energy ACCEPT and TRANSMIT (for OPERATING)	AP					
		FC	Tension Rod	Torsion Rod	Screw & Nut	Linkage System: Chain	System: Piston-Tube-Piston	Coil with Soft-iron Core
8	Position of Organ (open/closed) INDICATE	Directly from movable part	Position of the Actuating Organ		With additional indicators	Optical (Position Pointer | Verbal Legend | Colour Coding)	Acoustic
9	Oil Throughput DISCHARGE	AP	Overflow			Pressure activated Closure Organ	Level Regulation
		FC	Vertical Tube with Weir edge	Tube or Wall with Hole		Spring loaded | Weight loaded — Pressure Valve	no auxiliary energy — Float regulation | with auxiliary energy — Mech., hydr. electr. level regulation
10	Oil at max. level OVERFLOW REGULATE	AP	Overflow --- --- etc.				
		FC	Edge --	Closely connected to Function 9, where this regulation is possible with the stated function-carriers			
11	Fixed Parts to Container CONNECT	AP	Direct Connection				Indirect
			Permanent			Removable	
		FC	Weld (Weld Joint)	Glue (Glue Joint)		Screw + Seal (Screw Thread) | Force Fit (Bolts Shrink Joint)	Gravitational (Streamline Flow)
7a	Energy ACCEPT	AP	Linear action organs			Rotating organs	
		FC					Wheel — Lever

8-9

A: Matrix of Relationships between Partial Organs:

Organ →

	1	2	3	4	5	6	7	8	9	10	11
1	▨	×	×	×	×	×	×	×			
2	×	▨									
3	×		▨				×				
4	(×)	×		▨							
5	×				▨	×	×				
6	×				×	▨					
7	×		×		×	×	▨				
8	×				×			▨			
9									▨	×	
10									×	▨	
11									×	×	▨

↳ Organ marked in each <u>row</u> has relationship to organs of <u>column</u> label. Note: Some of these relationships are NOT mutual (bi-directional)

B: Abstract Organ Structure with basic Relationships:

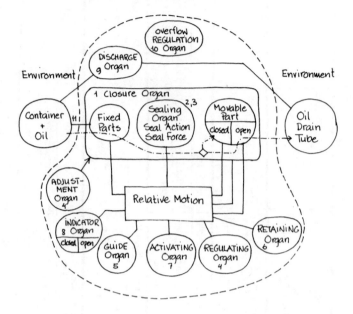

8-10 Concept 1:

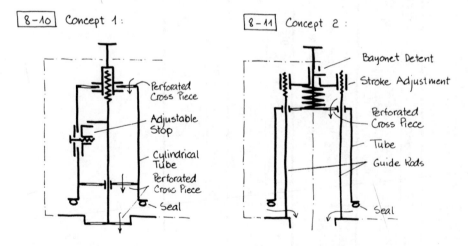

Perforated Cross Piece
Adjustable Stop
Cylindrical Tube
Perforated Cross Piece
Seal

8-11 Concept 2:

Bayonet Detent
Stroke Adjustment
Perforated Cross Piece
Tube
Guide Rods
Seal

is needed here between ease of representing the candidate solutions and ease of generating alternatives.]

3.5 Σ Concepts
Improve   Evaluate, decide   Verify

A coarse evaluation using four criteria in the usage categories and one for expenditure is shown in Figure 8-15. Variants 2, 3 and 4 have been given good

assessments, and are taken further in the design process.

Optimal concept

4 Aim: establish the preliminary layouts

This case study treats a fairly simple structure, in which the designer's thoughts in the conceptual phase

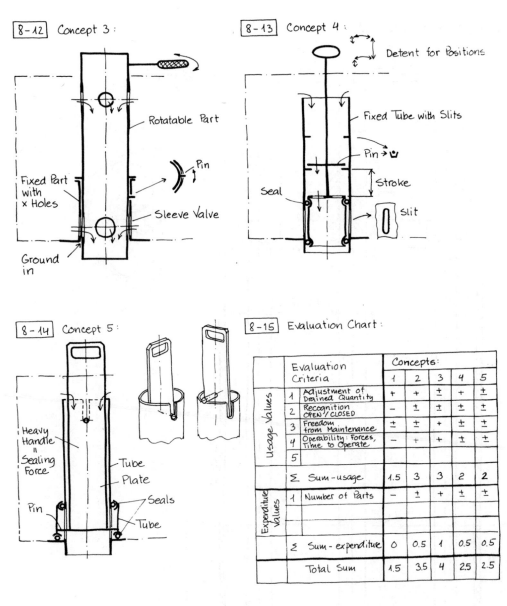

8-12 Concept 3:

Rotatable Part

Fixed Part with x Holes

Pin

Sleeve Valve

Ground in

8-13 Concept 4:

Detent for Positions

Fixed Tube with Slits

Pin

Stroke

Seal

Slit

8-14 Concept 5:

Heavy Handle = Sealing Force

Pin

Tube
Plate
Seals
Tube

8-15 Evaluation Chart:

		Evaluation Criteria	Concepts:				
			1	2	3	4	5
Usage Values	1	Adjustment of Drained Quantity	+	+	±	+	±
	2	Recognition OPEN // CLOSED	–	±	±	±	±
	3	Freedom from Maintenance	±	±	+	±	±
	4	Operability: Forces, Time to Operate	–	+	+	±	±
	5						
	Σ	Sum – usage	1.5	3	3	2	2
Expenditure Values	1	Number of Parts	–	±	+	±	±
	Σ	Sum – expenditure	0	0.5	1	0.5	0.5
		Total Sum	1.5	3.5	4	2.5	2.5

reached an unusually concrete level. The concept sketches are sufficiently detailed to act as preliminary layouts. Therefore the design team concludes that the whole of this phase can be omitted, and a direct entry into the dimensional layout phase is possible. This procedure also allows a direct comparison with the layout delivered with the problem assignment (Figure 8-3).

4.1 Establish the orientation points for form determination

4.2 Establish the arrangements, investigate re-use, rough form-giving, partial dimensioning

4.3 Establish types of material, classes of manufacturing method, tolerances and surface properties where necessary

4.4 Investigate the critical form-determination zones

4.5 Represent the preliminary layouts

Dimensional Layout

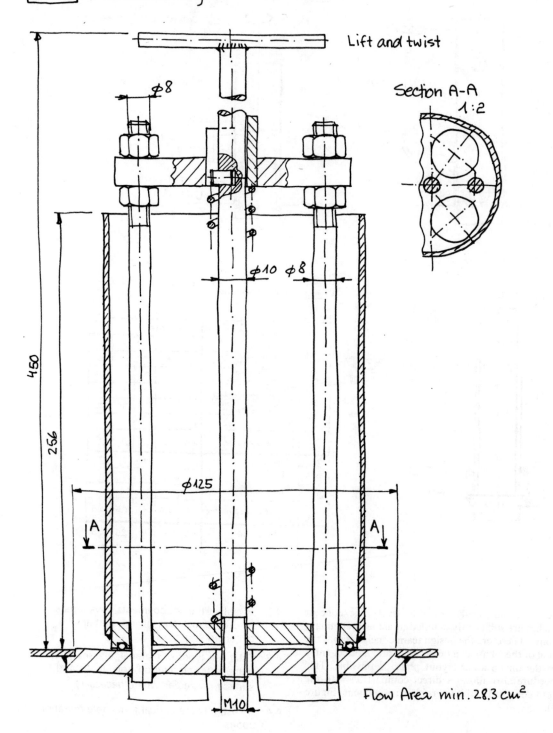

Lift and twist

Section A-A
1:2

Flow Area min. 28.3 cm²

8-17 Dimensional Layout

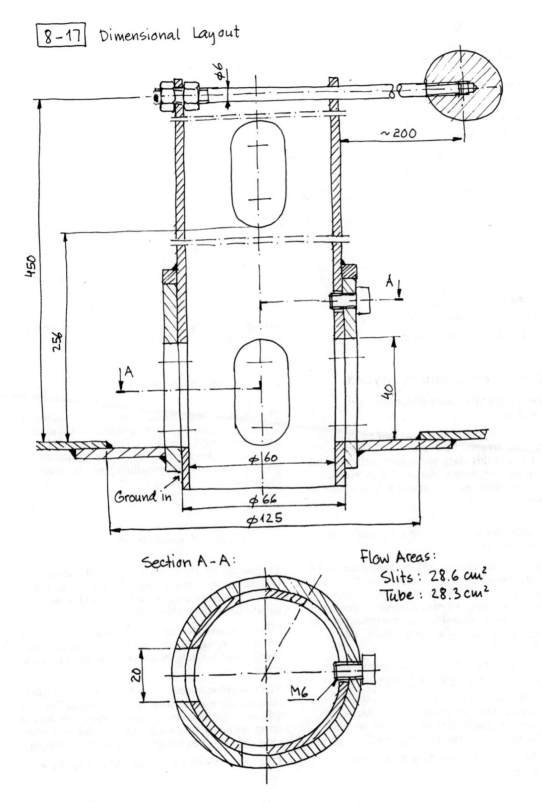

Section A-A:

Flow Areas:
Slits: 28.6 cm²
Tube: 28.3 cm²

M6

8-18	Evaluation Chart:				

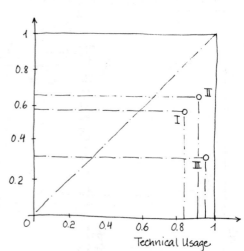

	Evaluation Criteria:	Ideal	Layout: I Fig.8-16	II Fig.8-17	III Fig.8-3
Usage Values	Ease of Use	4	4	4	4
	Recognition OPEN/CLOSE	4	4	3	3
	Adjustment of Valve position	4	4	4	4
	Adjustment of sealing force	4	3	3	4
	Ease of maintenance	4	3	4	4
	Limitation of valve movement	4	2	4	4
	Σ	24	20	22	23
	Techn. Rel. Value	1	0.83	0.91	0.95
Expenditure	Structural simplicity	4	3	4	2
	Ease of manufacture	4	4	4	2
	Σ	8	7	8	4
	Econ. Rel. Value	1	0.88	1.0	0.50

4.6   Σ Preliminary layout
      Improve   Evaluate, decide   Verify

Steps 4.1 to 4.6 are omitted for this case.

Optimum preliminary layout

5   Aim: establish the dimensional layouts

Many of the important decisions leading up to the dimensional layouts were taken in earlier steps. Variant 3 is at this stage particularly well prepared and relatively very simple. Variant 2 gives wide scope for a variety of forms, many of which should prove to be sound.

5.1   Deliver the substantiation for certain design characteristics

Certain design features and characteristics need to be reviewed, particularly with respect to their use. Decisions must be taken about suitable shapes and sizes of the openings to ensure adequate flow rates and sealing, accomplished for instance in variant 3 by overlapping the edges of the flow channel slits.

5.2   Establish the definitive arrangement, form determination, partial dimensioning

5.3   Establish the definitive and complete determination of materials, manufacturing methods, partial definitive determination of tolerances and surface properties

5.4   Optimize the critical form determination zones

Comments refer to combined use of steps 5.2 to 5.4.

Variant 3 has scope for improvement, particularly in the adjustment of the oil flow.

5.5   Represent the dimensional layouts

The resulting dimensional layouts are shown in Figures 8-16 and 8-17, corresponding to Concepts 2 and 3 (Figures 8-11 and 8-13). The first layout, Figure 8-3, should also be included in the evaluations to provide a basis for comparison and to assess the improvements.

5.6   Σ Dimensional layout
      Improve   Evaluate, decide   Verify

Evaluations of three newly generated variants are plotted on the relative strength diagram in Figure 8-19. The relative usage values are found to be about equal within reasonable limits.

[This is consistent with the previous work on this project, and should be generally true because only highly rated variants should proceed into the layout phase.]

The evaluation indicates that the original decision to redesign the existing solution was correct. The new solutions, particularly variant 3, show appreciably lower manufacturing costs than the original solution proposal. This was the declared aim of the project.

Concluding steps 6.1 to 6.7 are not developed for this case.

Index

abstract, -ion, 6, 43, 59, 97, 126
accept, 9
action location, xii, 8, 10, 77
active, 9, 64
aim, xii, xiv
alternatives, 1, 132
analysis, 6
approval, 6
arrangement, xiv, 33, 97
assigned, 1
automate, 38

black box, 7, 41
block schematic, 24, 75, 125
bought-out, 15, 57
boundaries, 7, 125

calculation, 55, 18
checking, 14
classes, 12
combination, 12
communication, xii
compatible, -ility, 13, 33, 80, 128
complexity, 22
component, 15, 97
concept, xiv, 9, 13, 14, 33, 112, 118, 119, 133
conceptualizing, 51, 123
conclusion, 7, 75
connecting, 77
constraints, xiv, 1
contract, 1, 22
control, 9, 70, 92, 125
cost, 20, 21
creative, -ity, ix, xii, 1, 30, 51, 57, 126
criteria, xiv, 1, 19, 33, 80, 82, 90, 99, 123, 132

decision, xii, 6, 14
description, ix
design characteristic, ix, x, 19
design document, ix, xii
design methodology, ix
design process, ix
design properties, 15
design specification, 1, 22
detail drawing, 18
development, 21
difficulty, 22
duty, xii, 7

effect, xii, xiv, 6, 7, 9, 19, 24, 44, 129
effector, xii
elaborate, 99

element, xii, xiv, 9, 15, 17
    constructional, xiv, 15, 17
    machine, 9, 15
embodiment, 99
environment, 9, 24
evaluate, 1, 6, 9, 14, 123
event, 1
execution, 7
expenditure, 33, 80, 82, 132
experience, xii

favourable, 9
feasible, 1, 57
form, 15, 129
freeze, 20
function, xii, xiv, 6, 8, 9, 19, 44, 51, 64, 75, 97, 110, 112, 125
    auxiliary, 9, 125
    control, 9, 125
    propulsion, 9, 125
    regulating, 9
function tree, 28, 75, 125
function-carrier, 8, 9, 10, 12, 30, 44, 70, 77, 88, 97, 126, 128

heuristic, 7
human operator, 7

implied fact, 1
improving, 14
information, ix, 1
input, xii, 10, 64
interaction, xii
iterative, -ion, ix, 16, 88

justify, 18

knowledge, xii, 7

layout, 13, 15, 19, 36, 82, 123, 133
    dimensional, 36
    preliminary, 82, 133
list of requirements, 1, 22, 75, 123

managed, 6
meaning, xii
mechanize, 38
method, -ology, ix, xii, xiv
mode of action, xii, 10, 12, 59, 64
model, ix, xiv, 88
morphological matrix, 12, 28, 64, 77, 93, 126

natural phenomena, 7

operand, xii, 6, 7, 24, 75
operation, xii, xiv, 7, 75, 91
operator, xii, 24
optimal, -um, ix, xiv, 7
order of magnitude, 106
organ, xiv, 8, 9, 10, 44, 77
output, 10, 64

passive, 9, 64
performance, xii, 1
plan, ix, 6, 67
point scoring/rating, 14, 82
preparation, ix, 7, 75
principle, 7, 9, 28, 30, 44, 77, 90, 91, 93, 94, 119, 123, 125
    technological, 7, 44, 90, 91, 93, 94, 123
    working, 9
priorities, 1
problem, -solving, 1, 58
procedure, -al, ix, xiv, 67, 88
process, ix, xii, 6, 7, 24
properties, 1, 15, 106, 110, 125
prototype, 21

quality, 14, 106

realized, 1
receptor, xii
records, ix
regulating, 9, 92
relationship, 9, 14, 128
relative strength, 14, 82, 136
represent, ix, xiv, 9, 17, 59, 125, 132
result, xii
re-use, 15
review, ix, 18

safety, 72
solution, ix
sponsor, 1
standard part, 15
state, ix, xii
state of the art, 15, 41
steps, xii, xiv, 1
strategy, ix, xii
structure, 6, 9, 13, 15, 17, 28, 70, 88, 93, 125, 126, 128
    anatomical, 9, 13, 15, 17
    functional, 9, 28, 70, 88, 93, 125, 126
    organ, 128
symbol, xiv
synthesize, 80

137